September, 2021

Mr. Ralph W. Curtin
CHD

"Every now and then God chooses to plant someone on our planet with an extra measure of capacity and insight. Without question, Will Mancini is one such person. *Future Church* is more than a must-read. With the cosmic shifts we have experienced recently, the church must pivot to a new normal to remain relevant. This book provides the road map."

Randy Frazee, pastor, Westside Family Church, and author of *The Connecting Church 2.0*

"Will Mancini once again demonstrates a characteristic genius in helping churches and denominations to recalibrate around essentials, to recover their distinctive callings, and so to find wholesale renewal. A rare and timely gift."

Alan Hirsch, author and activist

"*Future Church* is a fascinating consideration of why the church in North America has failed to create multiplying, disciples-making-disciples communities. Will Mancini and his team have been a consistently helpful guide to us for many years on creating good church culture. *Future Church* will help you grow this culture in your ministry as well!"

J. D. Greear, pastor, The Summit Church

"Will Mancini is one of the leaders I learn from and a thinker whose insights I trust. Smart leaders will dive into what Will has to say about the future church."

Carey Nieuwhof, founding pastor, Connexus Church, and host of *The Carey Nieuwhof Leadership Podcast*

"Through the years, Will Mancini has challenged me and the church I pastor to think deeply and critically about the church and its mission. This book adds to the list of tremendously helpful resources from Will, teaching us how to engage in the mission strategically and faithfully in the twenty-first century."

Vance Pitman, senior pastor, Hope Church Las Vegas

"Most church leaders I work with have been wrestling with a gnawing feeling that something needs to shift in our churches. Are we truly making disciples or just entertaining followers? What should we be measuring? How do we know we're accomplishing our mission? *Future Church* is an essential read for every church leader who is committed to defining real growth in a new era of ministry leadership."

Jenni Catron, leadership coach and founder of The 4Sight Group

"*Future Church* is an important and timely book for advancing the cause of reproducing disciples in the church. Let Will Mancini guide you into deeper thinking about Jesus's mission and more imaginative leadership for these challenging days ahead."

Dave Ferguson, lead pastor, Community Christian Church, and author of *Hero Maker: Five Essential Practices for Leaders to Multiply Leaders*

"Will and Cory have delivered an intelligent, imaginative, biblical journey, inviting followers of Jesus to a fresh disciple-making partnership. Paradigms and procedures that I've been suspicious of for a long time are exposed throughout this book. I can now see the future in a new light."

Stan Endicott, cofounder and chief culture officer, The Slingshot Group, and coauthor of *Improv Leadership: How to Lead Well in Every Moment*

"If you want to know what the future of the church is going to look like, read this book. Will is not only one of the most future-minded leaders I know, he's also deeply informed about past and present church practice. His ability to see and systematize the shift that is coming is impeccable. This is going to become required reading for my entire leadership team."

Daniel Im, pastor, Beulah Alliance Church, and author of *No Silver Bullets: 5 Small Shifts That Will Transform Your Ministry*

"*Future Church* is a master class in Real Church. Don't read this for ideas, insights, and initiatives that last a day or a week. Enroll your mind in this book for thoughts and tasks that linger and lead for a lifetime. Every page will challenge, delight, inspire, and deepen your church and raise your game."

Leonard Sweet, author, professor, and founder of Preach the Story

"*Future Church* invites twenty-first-century followers of Jesus to re-anchor in the ancient charter of a radically missional movement. The book navigates the polarity of church models mired in well-intended handicaps by offering refreshing *tertium quid*–type clarity on what could be, what must be. As a constructive plea, *Future Church*'s experience-based frameworks and principles invite leaders to reject the enduring growth limitations of yesterday's compromised models for breakthroughs today."

Mike Sharrow, CEO, The C12 Group

FUTURE CHURCH

SEVEN LAWS
OF REAL CHURCH GROWTH

WILL MANCINI
AND CORY HARTMAN

BakerBooks

a division of Baker Publishing Group
Grand Rapids, Michigan

Published by Baker Books
a division of Baker Publishing Group
PO Box 6287, Grand Rapids, MI 49516-6287
www.bakerbooks.com

Printed in the United States of America

Library of Congress Cataloging-in-Publication Data
Names: Mancini, Will, 1969– author. | Hartman, Cory, author.
Title: Future church : seven laws of real church growth / William Mancini and Cory
    Hartman.
Description: Grand Rapids, Michigan : Baker Books, a division of Baker Publishing
    Group, 2020.
Identifiers: LCCN 2020024578 | ISBN 9781540900616
Subjects: LCSH: Church growth. | Discipling (Christianity)
Classification: LCC BV652.25 .M185 2020 | DDC 253—dc23
LC record available at https://lccn.loc.gov/2020024578

The names and details of the people and situations described in this
book have been changed or presented in composite form in order
to ensure the privacy of those with whom the authors have worked.

The author is represented by the literary agency of The Gates Group.

21 22 23 24 25 26   7 6 5 4 3

Will dedicates this book to his father and mother, William and Leila Mancini, who model Future Church by being faithful to the organized expression of church over a lifetime without compromising fervent relational disciple making, even when the church didn't acknowledge it.

Cory dedicates this book to his children, Jack, Orphie, Arwen, and Israel, disciples of Future Church.

CONTENTS

FOREWORD

I n January 2020, I read about a virus in Wuhan, China. I'm not sure exactly why, but I thought at the time this might be something big.

I began telling people in February we were going to see schools and churches close, and we would tell our grandchildren one day about this spring. People were pretty skeptical—for about a month.

Since I started preparing my staff at the Billy Graham Center at Wheaton College in February for the coming virus, we were ready to provide a number of resources to churches early on when the pandemic hit.

I was probably patting myself on the back for my foresight when Donna, my wife, asked me, "So, if you saw this coming, why did you leave our retirement in the stock market?"

She was right. I did not see what I needed to see. And probably the only reason that I even took the virus seriously at first was I had watched the movie *Contagion* over the Christmas holidays.

You see, telling the future about anything is hard. Telling the future about culture is hard, and discerning the future church might be even harder. There are three things that we might want to consider as we think about the future of the church.

First, *patterns are hard to break.*

Even in the pandemic, churches discovered pretty quickly how hard it is to adjust to a dramatically different reality. Our church life, Sunday services, organizational approach, and general patterns of worship have really not changed that much for a generation.

Suddenly, every pastor in America became a televangelist. Ministers who resisted streaming their services suddenly embraced the technology; some who had criticized online services found themselves doing them. The coronavirus forced rapid change for a season.

However, my bigger concern is not that things will all change. It is that things will go back to the way they were. That's what happened during wars and economic downturns for centuries. The best predictor of the future is the immediate past. The best predictor of future behavior is past behavior.

If we are going to see God's people fully unleashed for God's mission, it will take some pattern breaking, and that's hard.

But the possibility for change is the greatest in tumultuous times. Things that have been building, perhaps unnoticed in the grind of day-to-day life, suddenly seem to accelerate in seasons of uncertainty. And the hope of real change is, I think, before us today.

Second, *change builds but then surprises us.*

As change accelerates there are breakthrough moments. Tipping points, some call them. There was John Huss and other dissenters who had concerns about the established church, and suddenly there's the swing of a hammer and Ninety-Five Theses are nailed on a church door. At that moment things tipped and the Protestant Reformation broke through.

We may be in one of those moments in regard to the church and its mission. We need to lean into the moment to see how God is moving in our midst.

Movements seem to spread out of nowhere, but their flood is preceded by tributaries preparing the way. What started as local change then becomes widespread in its impact.

We are in unprecedented times, yet none of this has caught God by surprise. He is the God of moments and movements.

What you will read in *Future Church* will help you perceive the movements breaking through our current moment. Will Mancini has seen a number of breakthrough moments in churches just like yours. Let his wisdom help you ride the wave of change.

Because that's what leaders do.

Finally, *leaders play a major role in change.*

Leaders give courage and guidance to ride these waves of change. This is why the early adopters and early majority play such a huge role in the diffusion of innovation, whether it's Apple computers with people like Steve Jobs or the rise of contemporary worship through places like Calvary Chapel.

We may be in one of those moments. It's a tumultuous time, and tumult is a catalyst for change. This is where Will Mancini and Cory Hartman's book can help us. In *Future Church*, you will read about the Seven Laws of Real Church Growth. At the heart of this is the question: What will you do with this ministry moment? Will is especially equipped to lead us in a moment like this.

We are never going back to the status quo before 2020 and COVID-19. That much is clear. What is less clear is how you will lead moving forward. In the following pages you will see not how to endure this season with a survivor's mindset but how to lead your church to its greatest disciple-making capacity in its history.

Since you are reading this book, you are thinking about the future. That's good. You won't get it all right, as my wife reminded me, but you can be better prepared for that moment of change.

Will began writing this book before the pandemic hit to help leaders look at the next twenty years of ministry. This year's events only accelerate the need for principles like he explains in these pages. You can lead the people God called you to lead, and this book can help you lead well.

Ed Stetzer, professor and dean at Wheaton College and executive
director of the Wheaton College Billy Graham Center

INTRODUCTION

Every Church's Primary Problem Today

On a single day not long ago, I (Will) spoke in two different cities with two very different pastors who put their
finger on the exact same problem. After ten thousand
conversations with pastors, two simple and unexpected statements converged with spontaneous and unbelievable insight. The
convergence was as rare and unforgettable as a solar eclipse, only
the effect was not a literal blocking of light but quite the opposite.
The statements became a portal to see the future of the church.

I spent the first half of the day with the sixty-five-year-old pastor
of one of the most successful Presbyterian churches in the country
(according to attendance and giving standards, of course). This
good man served the Lord well over his ministry and was now
transitioning to a new life stage. Yet as he reflected on a lifetime
of preaching, he privately expressed his quietly smoldering discontent about the condition of his church. "Will," he told me earnestly,
"the church has got to be more than the Rotary Club with a choir."

After this conversation I hopped on a plane to another city.
A thirty-five-year-old, newly minted lead pastor picked me up at
the airport. He was still enjoying the favor that comes from the

honeymoon phase of a pastoral tenure at his growing, midsized Baptist church. There was much excitement about the future in his congregation. In the car I asked him about his number one challenge. "Will," he replied, "*I have to convince my people that church is more than a show on Sunday with a few hooks in the water throughout the week.*"

And there it was: the beating heart of two passionate pastors testifying to the stopped heart of Jesus's mission in the organized church. The problem was not conveyed as a meteor-colliding crisis but as the pervasive pressing concern. The short phrases revealed at least five metaphors for the church: business, club, entertainment, performance, and bait on a hook. I don't think the young pastor had ever been to a Rotary Club, and I don't think the retiring pastor had ever fished with a trotline. But they were certainly on the same page.

Two successful pastors—almost two generations removed in ministry experience, on opposite ends of the theological and stylistic spectrum—articulated the exact same problem. They lead churches that by all accounts are thriving, but they secretly suspect that many of their people have little clue about the church Jesus actually started. People come to church but don't "get" church. The churches they serve feel like a pseudochurch. Something is missing.

My conversations that day revealed to me an extraordinary fact: it took one generation in time (from 2000 to 2020) for every generation of church leader in every faith tribe to feel the same primary problem—namely, that the church in North America is dramatically overprogrammed and underdiscipled. Of course, this challenge has been expressed at many other times in many different ways. But in our moment the named problem carries an unprecedented gravity and rings with piercing clarity. It is more than the observation of those gifted to be innovators or a

> The church in North America is dramatically overprogrammed and underdiscipled.

courageous few. Instead, every pastor has begun to ask themselves with greater freedom and conviction, "Are we making disciples or faking them?"

Leaders like the two pastors I talked to feel the expectations of Church As We Know It weighing down upon them, but the pressures do not line up with what they are truly called to do. That's what *Future Church* is all about: returning the organized church to the passionate conviction of disciple making in the way of Jesus.

To state the problem in its purest form I will articulate the substitute mission of the church that these two pastors are trying to correct. Think of this as the actual aim of local churches across the land that have so normalized mission drift that magnetic north barely registers on the compass. The functional Great Commission in North American churches has become:

Go into all the world and make more worship attenders, baptizing them in the name of small groups and teaching them to volunteer a few hours a month.

The purpose of *Future Church* is to provide a pathway that does not abandon the church to its current trajectory but boldly hails the need and reveals the opportunity to reset our compass in our cultural moment.

The *Future Church* Journey

Before we get started, I want to explain the authorship and the voice of this book. *Future Church* was coauthored by myself and my friend Cory Hartman, a writer and pastor. This book comes from both of us, and our ideas weave together throughout. Yet to make for a smoother and simpler reading experience, the book is written as if spoken by me individually. You can think of me as your guide on a journey crafted by us both.

To best help you, I start by escorting you uncomfortably deep into this problem that we are all familiar with but often do not fully understand. In order to awaken clarity and activate progress, I paint the contrast between faking disciples and making disciples in the church today. My goal is not to be simplistic or sassy but to apply my missional heartbeat and prophetic voice with a bit of grit. It has been said that prescription without diagnosis is malpractice. I want you to gain new appreciation for the breadth and depth of the dilemma. But I walk you deep down in order to lift you higher up—up with new vision and up with renewed conviction. There is a solution on the other side.

The journey of this book can be mapped this way:

- One problem
- Two rooms
- Three churches
- Seven laws
- One master tool

That is:

- **One problem** of faking disciples—the primary problem of every church today
- **Two rooms**—a simple picture that both unveils today's crisis in the North American church story and gives you help and hope for your church's story
- **Three churches** that when seen together become the most useful typology for understanding the North American church over the next twenty years
- **Seven laws** of organized disciple making for real church growth
- **One master tool** to map the way forward, which consists of **two funnels** derived from the modern ministry model and Jesus's multiplication model

I got the idea for a book on Future Church when my thoughts startled me awake in the dark, quiet hours one night in 2016. Four years later, when we were putting the finishing touches on our first draft in the spring of 2020, many churches had stopped meeting for public worship because the COVID-19 pandemic had struck North America.

It astounds me that this book was being finalized under these circumstances. All of us had been hearing for a long time that the future was coming fast. But while this was being written, change overtook the church at supersonic speed. It felt like we passed from 2020 to 2030 overnight.

I realize that it's foolhardy to make sweeping predictions about something I am still living through in July 2020. Still, from this vantage point, I believe that the COVID pandemic probably constitutes the greatest innovation opportunity that leaders will have in a lifetime. Yet there is a danger that the church will miss the moment.

Shortly after the pandemic froze life as we knew it, my friend Neil Cole gave me perhaps the best way of thinking about the crisis as it pertains to the church. Neil said that COVID-19 is a shot across the bow of cultural Christianity. He meant that our inability to gather in customary fashion for weekend worship had the potential to dislocate and purge the lasting remnants of a Christianity rooted in local culture and social custom instead of a conviction to follow Jesus.

A warning shot is scary, but it's also gracious, just as God's confusion of the languages at Babel was a scary act of grace. In Genesis 1:28, God commissioned the human race to "be fruitful and increase in number; fill the earth and subdue it." By Genesis 11, the human race was failing to obey the instruction. Instead of spreading out as instructed, people clustered together to make a name for themselves and rival God. With forceful mercy, God disrupted their construction to reengage their commission.

In similar fashion, the coronavirus forcibly and lovingly reveals what is true about the church in the early twenty-first century and offers us the chance to renew our obedience to the Great Commission. When a church can't cluster together for weekend programming, it shows how faithful it is to the mission when it's scattered.

Meanwhile, every week of the pandemic we have been flooded by a hot mess of tips and tactics for how the church should respond. As useful as these might be for making quick fixes to keep things rattling along, they don't address the much greater vulnerabilities the pandemic exposes. At best they help leaders adapt, but they don't help them innovate.

Imagine, for instance, that the internet breaks tomorrow. The chaos it would wreak on the world would make COVID look like child's play. In addition, almost all the advice for church leaders on how to cope with the pandemic would become completely irrelevant overnight.

Yet, whether a pandemic strikes or the internet breaks or the church is driven into hiding, not a single word of this book you are holding would become irrelevant. Its principles were relevant before we sat down to write them, they're relevant today, and we believe they will remain relevant in all circumstances until Christ returns. The church may be closed on weekends, but the mission of Jesus is never boarded up. The internet could disappear, but the word of God would still sound to the ends of the earth (Ps. 19:4).

> The church may be closed on weekends, but the mission of Jesus is never boarded up.

This book begins by displaying the problem the church is mired in, but it ends by revealing the wonder of the mission that Christ has called us to. Our reason for journeying is to see the restoration of a body as old as the apostles and as new as tomorrow, whatever tomorrow holds. Welcome to Future Church.

PART 1

FAKING DISCIPLES

THE UNCOMFORTABLE REALITY OF LOWER ROOM LEADERSHIP

TWO ROOMS

The Best Picture to Expose the North American Church's Greatest Challenge

One of my favorite things about being a ministry consultant is that I get to meet a lot of people with interests and hobbies I never would have imagined. In recent months I met a pastor who collects chess sets from across the world, a denominational leader who hunts wild boar with a knife, and a missionary who makes guitars out of cigar boxes.

In comparison, my hobbies are a bit more conventional. I like Mexican food, snowboarding, looking at real estate, and fishing for smallmouth bass on a flowing river. But if I have a quirky hobby, it's this: I love useful tools that show important ideas *through pictures.*

Okay, I know that makes me kind of a nerd. But I love pictures; I can't get enough of them. I am an avid Instagrammer. My favorite part of writing a blog post might be picking the stock photos to go with it. I *do* judge a book by its cover (at first), and when I get a new book, the first thing I do is flip through to find the pictures. I am a super visual person, and I enjoy helping others engage the power of visual thinking.

So, as a consultant and author, I am known as a toolmaker—not the kind of tool you hang on a pegboard in your garage but the kind you draw on the whiteboard in your office. I enjoy creating visual presentations of important ideas to create new perspective, deeper understanding, and ultimately permanent breakthrough. I have been doing this for twenty years and have made many tools that I love sharing with people in my books. But the visual tool I made that has done the most good for the most leaders over two decades of consulting has never been seen in print—until now.

The Four Most Common Reasons People Attach to a Church

The picture-tool begins with a question: *Why do people call your church "home"?* Phrased another way, *What connects people emotionally to your church?* If you could roll a soul X-ray machine in front of a person to see the real answer to that question, what would light up in their heart? I have found that most people in most churches answer with a combination of the following four attachments.

1. Place

Some people are emotionally tied to the church's physical structure because of its convenient location, its architectural beauty, or their personal investment in dollars and sweat to keep it in good shape over the years. To them, in a real way, the facility is the church. Whether it's a hip industrial campus downtown, a fabulous strip mall renovation, a suburban big box that would make AMC envious, or a beautiful steeple with a dash of stained glass in the rural countryside, we make our places and then our places make us. If you want to know how strong *place* is as a connection dynamic, just mention relocation in the next church business meeting.

A film roll of stories spins through my mind when I think of the role of place. One church in Amarillo, Texas, had so many donated-by signs on church fixtures that even the air conditioner condenser unit in the backyard had a plaque on it. I thought to myself, "This church can't even upgrade its A/C without offending someone!"

Perhaps the most dramatic personal experience with place for me came when the Willowdale Chapel near Chadds Ford, Pennsylvania, called Auxano about ten years ago. The leadership at that time reached out for my help without realizing that it was my home church when I was in high school. I was going back to consult the church where I attended youth group and preached my first sermon. The most wonderful part of my first day back on the property came not when I took in the impressive worship center that had been built to accommodate growth since my day. It was when I walked into the dingy, cinder-block Sunday school rooms in the basement of the original chapel. A flood of memories came back with the familiar sights and smells of those small classrooms. I was instantly reminded of spiritual breakthroughs and meaningful relationships. At that moment I would have fiercely resisted any suggested changes to the basement because of my sentimental connection alone.

2. Personality

Some people are emotionally connected to a particular leader because of their amazing skill as a communicator, wisdom as a Bible teacher, or compassion in the ups and downs of life. To these people, the leader is the church. If you want to know how strong *personality* is, imagine how attendance would be impacted if your senior pastor suddenly announced he was leaving for a year, and that a guest preacher would be speaking the next fifty-two weeks.

One dramatic illustration of this is a stellar leader who planted a church in a midsized Midwestern city. After twenty years of leadership, the fruit of his ministry was significant. For several years his church even registered on *Outreach*'s list of the one hundred fastest-growing churches. While we were traveling together, he confided in me that he had been diagnosed with Parkinson's disease. Several months later, still before the disease had made any noticeable impact on his physical presence, he announced his condition to the congregation. Within four months the church's average worship attendance dropped by over ten percent. The elders wrestled with what the root cause of the decline might be. They finally concluded, "People like a winner. And evidently you can't be winning if you have Parkinson's."

No matter how you slice it, people in a church are deeply connected to the staff of the church. Even when a relatively ineffective pastor leaves a church of any size, there are always a handful of folks who check out.

Before moving on, it is worthwhile to pause and look at place and personality in light of church history. These two Ps are essential to Church As We Know It, but they are incidental to real church growth. From AD 100 to 300, the Christian movement spread like wildfire despite hostile conditions. While we cannot know the numbers for sure, we know that it grew in order of magnitude from thousands of believers to millions of them. Rodney Stark conservatively estimates that in AD 300 there were six million believers who made up 10 percent of the population. Alan Hirsch observes that in this two-hundred-year stretch, there were no such things as dedicated church buildings (place) or professional clergy (personality). The persecuted church became a force in the world without the supposed advantages that we take for granted as necessities today.[1]

3. Programs

Some people are emotionally tied to the various activities and ways of doing things at church. This may be their favorite way of doing the Tuesday morning women's Bible study, their affection for home groups, missional communities, AWANA, kids' church, men's prayer breakfast, or how we make decisions as an elder board. To these people, the activities are the church. If you want to test someone's connection to a *program*, just mention that church leadership is considering upgrading their favorite one with a newer one.

Early in my consulting career I learned the power of emotional connection to program. I helped a church in Virginia launch a contemporary worship service. Everyone was on board that it needed to happen, but there was deep division about *when* it should happen. The old guard wanted to keep it an early service at the crack of dawn, but the pastor was ready to launch at prime time—the 11 a.m. slot. I came to a board meeting perfectly prepared with a sequence of questions to sell the eleven o'clock option.

In the room of a dozen leaders, I ended up engaging in dialogue with Deacon Jim with the full attention of the rest of the board. "Jim," I asked with quiet confidence, "if we launch the contemporary service at eleven o'clock, you do know that more families with young kids will attend, right?"

"Yep," he replied.

"And Jim," I continued, "you do know that some of those families will not have a saving knowledge of Jesus Christ, right?"

"Yep," he repeated.

"And Jim," I drove on, "you would gladly launch the contemporary service at the eleven o'clock time slot if you knew that an eight-year-old boy would find Jesus and a church home for the very first time, right?"

Jim didn't reply right away; instead, he looked reflectively into the distance. Then he finally spoke: "But I have been attending the traditional service since *I* was eight years old."

My jaw dropped in disbelief. Eventually the church launched a fledgling contemporary service at 8:30 a.m.

4. People

Some people are emotionally connected to their friends at church, the *people* who create an atmosphere of acceptance and first-name familiarity. It may be as simple as a fifteen-minute chat in the church entryway. Or it may be a solid, deep kinship in a long-running House Church. Or it may be somewhere in between like the warm connections amidst a yearlong weekday small group. For many, these interactions are the church. To measure the strength of this draw of people, imagine how a family may respond once they learn that their two best friends at church are relocating to another town. Would their connection to the church be threatened?

A funny feature of congregations is how people resist even small changes in worship service times. Let's say a church has two Sunday morning services at 9:30 and 11:00 a.m. As the church grows, an additional service time is required. Let's say the leadership decides to launch new service times at 9:00, 10:15, and 11:30 a.m. With additional service times you would think people would appreciate more options to suit their preference. But they don't. Church attenders resist the change because they resist the loss of the natural ebb and flow of friendships defined by the current schedule. Changing service times equates to "shuffling the relational deck" of the church. It might even boot you from your favorite auditorium seat or pew location with the invisible nameplate with your name etched on it.

I remind church leaders all the time that it's easier to find this kind of connection in a local bar than it is in a local church. It's a judgment-free zone where—cue the *Cheers* theme song— "everybody knows your name." All humans crave this whether they know it or not. And this sociological reality of life makes the world turn round whether a person is a believer or not. So when a person *does* find it at church, the last thing they want is to lose it.

At some point every effective disciple of Jesus must confront a natural tension. After a believer experiences salvation, the new saint will most likely experience some kind of biblical community, and many times it is downright wonderful. Yet, at some point, the believer will be confronted with the mission of Jesus, which presents a challenging question: "Is it more important to preserve the intimacy of the fellowship or to unsettle that familiarity and warmth in order to add the next outsider?" To say it another way, "Will I intentionally walk away from the good vibes of my small group in order to multiply the group so that others may join?" To say it Jesus's way, "Will I gladly leave the ninety-nine for the lost one?"

Generations of church experience testify to the challenge of the "us four and no more" Christian club. When people get their identity from friendships at church, they resist the proverbial open chair. As my friend Larry Osborne points out, most Christians are like LEGO blocks with all their connectors snapped together with other believers they already know.[2]

The Most Important Picture of Twenty Years of Consulting

Now that we have surveyed the four Ps, take a moment to picture the church as a two-story house. When people come into your church for the first time, what draws them in? When they decide to stick around the church, what moves them to make themselves at home? The answer to both is usually the four Ps of place, personality, programs, and people. Just as a person usually enters a house at ground level, people enter your church by walking into what I call the *Lower Room*, where the church's four Ps are located.

When people engage with a church, they necessarily form opinions about the place, the personality, the programs, and the people. They cannot help but make or not make an immediate connection to all of the obvious things around them. These are the concrete things they can see and touch and will like or dislike. If someone talks about why they like a church, one of the four Ps usually takes center stage:

- **Place:** "The new building is close to where we live."
- **Personality:** "Pastor Carlos is such a good teacher."

- **Program:** "Emma and Aiden really love going to Kidz Zone."
- **People:** "It's the church our friends Joe and Sally attend."

Because every person coming in contact with a church first encounters its Lower Room, every church should aspire to have attractive Lower Room features. I want to see a stellar Lower Room in every church I work with. I want them to have amazing facilities. I want the people to think the pastor hung the moon. I hope the programs are exciting and dynamic. And, of course, I want people to have great chemistry with friends they enjoy.

It follows that good church leaders pay close attention to the Lower Room. In fact, in order to grow the church, leaders spend much time making their four Ps more accessible from the outside and more irresistible on the inside. We upgrade our sanctuary like we upgrade our kitchen. We hire a young associate pastor to attract younger families. We roll out a new sermon series like a new season on Netflix. We attempt to make our guests feel as welcome as VIPs at Disney World.

Please note that in the lifetimes of today's church leaders, this has been the tried and true formula for church growth: if you maximize the attractiveness of your place, the charisma of your personalities, the excellence of your programs, and the welcome of your people, your church will grow. It's that simple.

At the same time, however, there remains a disturbing question lurking in the house's shadow. Is capturing people in the Lower Room *real* church growth? Is this what Christ called us to do: tie people emotionally to a place, personalities, programs, and people? Does a church where most people are most attached to facility, leaders, activities, and relational chemistry correspond to what the church *is* according to the Bible?

Of course it's not! Jesus gave *every* church a dynamic mission and *each* church one-of-a-kind potential. In addition, people prefer to be emotionally connected to a much bigger idea, a more transcendent cause. The life that Jesus offers to each of his disciples through this amazing thing called the local church can hardly be captured in *the Lower Room alone.*

We need another room. I call it the *Upper Room*, and it changes everything.

The Upper Room

The Upper Room offers an alternative answer to the question "Why do the people in your church call it 'home'?" People in the Upper Room are emotionally attached to a sense of purpose beyond place, personalities, programs, and people. Being in the Upper Room means that a person knows and names *God's unique disciple-making vision for a church.*

Figure 1 – Two Different Motivations for Church Attenders

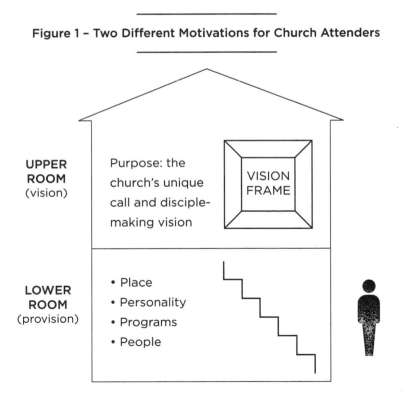

People in the Upper Room not only like the vision but have fallen in love with it. Imagine a Jesus-following college girl excited about her new boyfriend. Picture her sharing with close friends all about his charming personality and commitment to God as she beams with a sense of attraction. Now imagine a church attender excited to share about her church in a similar way, talking up the specific dream of the church's gospel impact. People in the Upper Room call their church home because they are passionate about how God wants to use their church family as it gathers regularly and scatters daily. Most importantly, they have given themselves to this holy cause, wholly.

Let's evaluate the two rooms through a simple comparison. If you were to ask an eight-year-old boy what he wanted most for his life, every answer would be tangible: an electric scooter, a PlayStation, et cetera. But if you were to ask the parents of the eight-year-old boy what they wanted most for their son, every answer would be intangible: a vital relationship with God, acceptance, confidence, and so on. We wouldn't really fault the boy for wanting the next best toy. But we would find the parents alarmingly myopic if not downright irresponsible if they aimed at a tangible thing. Why? Because it would completely miss the beauty and opportunity of being human. We might say the boy is emotionally connected to a Lower Room of life while his mature parents live in the Upper Room.

Here is another way to look at it: what quality do place, personalities, programs, and people have in common? *They change.* And not only do they change, but virtually every leader understands that they *must change* over time to ensure the viability of both the organization and its higher purpose. The building needs remodeling. The pastor retires. Programs get tired. People move away.

Think of this incredible advantage of the Upper Room: even when the place, personalities, programs, and people in the Lower Room change or fall away, the commitment of Upper Room people does not waver. In fact, I have routinely seen the conversion of people who used to resist change now insisting on it. The secret is this: people don't resist change; they resist loss. (If you offer someone a 15 percent raise today, chances are they will not resist the change!) If people are emotionally connected to the Upper Room, they don't have anything to lose when the Lower Room changes. The four Ps do not compel them to claim the church as their own. Rather, Upper Room people truly identify with the church's Vison Frame—that is, its disciple-making mission and disciple-shaping values, worked out through its disciple-moving strategy toward disciple-defining measures of success in light of its disciple-inspiring vision.

> People don't resist change; they resist loss.

You will hear leaders in both the church and business world attest to this dynamic of change management. Andy Stanley teaches leaders to "marry your mission but only date your model" as he encourages them to adapt and update methodology.[3] In his classic book *Built to Last*, Jim Collins uses a yin-yang symbol to contrast a leader's relationship to continuity and change.[4] Organizations that endure must have an undying commitment to a core ideology on the one hand but a ruthless commitment to change everything else on the other. This ironically becomes the only way to stay true to your core. I put it this way when I talk to church leaders: the Upper Room is what you etch in marble, the Lower Room is what you write in the sand.

In the end, the supremacy of the Upper Room does not make the Lower Room a bad place, but it does put it in its place. The four Ps of the Lower Room are useful to bring people into an environment that supports disciples of Jesus, but disciples are not supposed to remain there. They do not truly become friends of Jesus who do what he commands (John 15:14) unless they ascend from the Lower Room to the Upper Room. The Lower Room is meant to draw people in, but the Upper Room is meant to draw people up. The Lower Room is the *pro*vision of the church, but the Upper Room must be the vision. The Lower Room can and will change; the Upper Room is enduring.

We can easily see both rooms in Jesus's ministry. When he feeds the five thousand men (a crowd that could have been up to twenty thousand men, women, and children), we see Jesus providing compelling teaching and miracle bread to the masses. It's a Lower Room environment. The Gospel of John testifies that people came primarily motivated by the benefits Jesus provided, which included a free Happy Meal for the kids. But at the end of Jesus's ministry, how many disciples are gathered who have signed their pledge card with ink not pencil? One window to this number is the 120 in the literal upper room recorded in Acts 1:15; another possibility is the five hundred Jesus appeared to at one time after the resurrection, according to Paul (1 Cor. 15:6). If you were to have asked Jesus, "How big is your church?" how would he have answered? I probably would have leaned toward the five-digit attendance figure, especially if I was reporting to my denomination. I think Jesus would have reported 120.

> If you were to have asked Jesus, "How big is your church?" how would he have answered?

Unfortunately, in many churches, including in churches that appear to be thriving, few people dwell in the Upper Room. When someone tells me they lead a big church, I immediately wonder which room they are talking about. I tend to see the attendance on weekends as the size of the Lower Room; it is the size of the immediate ministry opportunity, not the size of the church. The true size of the church is the Upper Room. I would rather lead an Upper Room church of 120 than a Lower Room church of 1,200. The first is a force in the community. The other is an event in the building.

Confessions of a Consultant

In 2001, I started consulting with churches full time and eventually launched an organization called Auxano. At that time I introduced a new process for helping each church articulate its unique disciple-making mission and model revolving around the concept of vision. Since then I founded the Future Church Company, comprising Younique, which delivers gospel-centered life planning to individual disciples; Denominee, which helps networks, multichurches, and denominations bring value to congregations; and Pivvot, which brings the principles of *Future Church* to the local church.

When I began helping churches overcome barriers to growth, I was thinking about more than merely accumulating attenders. Rather, I was thinking about real church growth born from the Word's effect on the human heart and developed through the pattern of disciple-making disciples—men and women who value, practice, and model new skills in living the way of Jesus.

For two decades my primary work has been to help each church assess, articulate, and advance how God has shaped it to make disciples according to its unique context, its one-of-a-kind congregational makeup, and the particular callings of its leaders. I call it Vision Framing. The goal in building a Vision Frame with a church team has nothing to do with an event-based retreat to articulate a new mission, vision, and values. Rather, it involves a disruptive and challenging process where the team rethinks its existence at a core level and remakes its church operating system from the ground up. My calling is all about applying essence; a Vision Framing process penetrates to the essence of a local church and pushes it through to application. Vision Framing isn't complete until the empowered local leadership can articulate with convictional clarity how they will live out their own disciple-making model *in their time* with a specific dream for dramatic gospel good *in their place*.

The Vision Frame answers five irreducible questions of clarity. These answers become the codified vocabulary that defines the Upper Room. First, this makes it accessible to people; vision transfers through people not paper. Second, it enables the church to reevaluate, realign, repurpose, replace, remove, or renovate the Lower Room stuff in order to promote and propel the Upper Room vision.

For as long as I and many others have been leading church teams through Vision Framing, we've never faced a lack of interest. The demand for our tools testifies to the church's hunger to make the main thing the main thing. Churches understand what it means to have no growth or fake growth; every church I have worked with wants real growth by making disciples of Jesus.

Yet I have a confession to make: some of our work has contributed more to the illusion of fluency in disciple making than it has to the real thing. If I could have seen this clearly as it was happening, I would have called it out. But in real time, my hopefulness overpromised on what my helpfulness delivered. With rearview mirror visibility on a twenty-year report card, I would sort my clients into three buckets: a leading third that soared in fulfilling the mission of Jesus, a middle third that demonstrably picked up the pace, and a lagging third that only messaged the mission—all talk, no do.

I now see that although no church—large or small, traditional or contemporary, Baptist or Presbyterian, mainline or new start— disagrees with Jesus's mandate for his church to make disciples, many fundamentally fail to do so *even while they become more adept at articulating disciple-making outcomes as their core reason for being.*

Words Create Worlds

I love the phrase "words create worlds," attributed to Abraham Joshua Heschel. That mantra expresses the conviction I bring to churches to help them name what they can do best as communities of disciple-making disciples. I am an idea architect and words are construction material. I often teach that the secret to getting people in the Upper Room is building a staircase, one that is not made of wood but of words—the shared, codified vocabulary of the Upper Room. Words are the leader's primary tool, after all. If we can just say it well, say it together, say it often, and say it with feeling, surely people will catch the vision; surely they will taste and see the biggest ideas of God!

This is my conviction, and I have found it to be the strength of my ministry. It works. But there is a weakness in overrelying on the technology of getting words right. Yes, words create worlds. Yes, the pen is mightier than the sword. But it's also true that talk is cheap.

I now understand more clearly how a church that is not making disciples can walk through an intensive Vision Framing process and come out the other side a spiffier-sounding church still not making disciples. Even when a church's disciple-making language improves, the Upper Room remains inaccessible.

I do not believe the Vision Frame has been fatally flawed; not only myself but also the consultants, denominational leaders, and pastors I've trained and certified have seen tremendous fruit. Yet I do believe that, as every reflective person and organization eventually discovers, our greatest strength carries with it our greatest weakness. In our case, we have helped people appreciate and even personalize the disciple-making *words* of Jesus, but that has not automatically propelled them into the disciple-making *works* of Jesus.

The bottom line is that I underestimated the power of the Lower Room. Its gravitational pull is not the tug of a minor moon but the force field of a black hole. Our consulting work is extensive, but it has not always broken through to the church's essence. When I thought I was installing a new operating system, some churches were merely installing a new app only to abandon it for the next silver-bullet app a year later.

The Seven Laws of the Upper Room as Visionary Planning Prequel

In my first clarity book, *Church Unique*, I unpacked the problem of photocopied ministry, and I unveiled the process of articulating a Vision Frame that enables church leaders to answer the five irreducible questions of organized disciple making for their unique congregation. The Vision Frame is an operating system designed to help leaders shape their church's culture and guide their church's growth. It helps a pastor lead from a unique disciple-making mission and model.

In my second clarity book, *God Dreams*, I showed church leaders how to discern and develop a long-range vision for their church and then install a simple execution plan to achieve it. Built on the Vision Frame, *God Dreams* features the Horizon Storyline (also known as the "1:4:1:4"), a tool that expands and deepens a church's answer to the fifth irreducible question, "Where is God taking us?" These books are volumes one and two of a visionary planning methodology used by churches of every faith tribe (see the appendix).[5]

When a Vision Framing process is done well, the end result is always one of a kind. This is what I live for. In all my years as a consultant, I have been Mr. Uniqueness. I have never lost my abiding passion to see each church (and, through my organization Younique, each individual believer) live out its special calling from God, to do what ten thousand other churches could never do. I urge churches not to short-circuit God's missional potential by cutting and pasting someone else's playbook. I designed the Vision Frame as the tool to help leaders know and name the beautiful, one-of-a-kind features of its Upper Room.

Yet I now see that all the work that goes into furnishing the Upper Room makes little difference if leaders are not acquainted with the Upper Room itself. If well-intentioned leaders are locked in a Lower Room mindset, all the great words they craft do not take people upstairs; they keep everyone, including themselves, circulating on the ground floor. They use more vivid, purpose-filled language to keep drawing people into the Lower Room, and they overlay Upper Room expectations onto Lower Room actions.

Consequently, before I walk a church team through the five irreducible questions of organized disciple making—the Vision Frame—it is not safe to assume that we all share the same convictions about disciple making that the Vision Frame is founded on. That means I have to introduce leaders to the Upper Room so that they commit to it themselves before I help them bring the rest of their church upstairs. So, when I walk into a church today, I no longer start with the five questions but with seven laws.

That's what *Future Church* is all about. *Future Church* is my first book on the church's general calling—the disciple-making principles that ought to characterize every church. This book does not describe a boilerplate ministry model to be imposed on every church. Rather, it describes the fundamentals that every church must hold and operationalize if its own unique model would take people where God yearns for them to go.

Think of *Future Church* as the prequel to *Church Unique* and *God Dreams*—the episode released later in the series that tells how the whole saga begins. I wish every pastor, church leader, and ministry I have ever served as a consultant could have read it before we started working together.

This is even truer today, because every church and leader in North America is at a crossroads. Over the next twenty years, each church will increasingly resemble one of three types. Which one yours becomes has everything to do with its Upper Room, its Lower Room, and where people's greater attachment lies.

THREE CHURCHES

The Most Useful Typology for the Next Twenty Years

The first day of my professional ministry career was also one of the worst. It happened at Clear Creek Community Church in February of 1998.

It was a Tuesday afternoon, and I finally got in touch with Dan, the lay leader responsible for our children's ministry team. It was an important call because that Thursday night we were having our weekly program team meeting and run-through. The church had recently moved from age-graded classrooms to a so-called kids' church philosophy; that made the Thursday meeting even more essential, because we were designing a full-blown worship service with homemade creative programming every week.

Obviously, that was a big job, but that's what attracted me to my new position. Bruce Wesley, the founding pastor, had recruited me as a potential church planter. He sold me on the idea that developing a children's ministry would be like planting a church within a church before I planted outside the church.

As I got to know Dan on the phone that day, I was increasingly excited that I could now step into a leadership role that would relieve some of his burden. I even remember thinking how fortunate the children's ministry was now to have a full-time pastor and trained seminarian at the helm. I was a bit unclear on the details of how the handoff would be made, but before it could happen Dan said something that shook me to the core. As the conversation was winding down, he did the unthinkable: he invited me to sit in on Thursday night's program team meeting *if I wanted to.*

If I wanted to? Are you kidding me? What was he thinking? He was the amateur, and it was clearly time for him to step aside, for me, the professional. I sat for one hour paralyzed at my desk. I thought to myself, "What in the world have I gotten myself into?" Then I thought, "How could I have accepted this assignment that would never utilize my special knowledge of Greek and my refined preaching skills?" Dan's invitation scandalized my professional ministry sensibility.

By God's grace, the Holy Spirit gave me a flash of hope that day. If I wasn't going to lead the program directly, I would have to do it indirectly. But what did that mean practically? The Holy Spirit woke me up to the fact that my job was not to lead a program but a person. The only clue to keep me going was an idea that rang like a bell in my mind: *my job is to lead the program by having lunch with Dan.* I didn't know if I could succeed, but I was willing to give it a try. No one had given me a playbook for it, but maybe I could figure it out.

I credit Bruce Wesley, Dan, and the whole leadership community of Clear Creek for modeling a healthier church culture than seminary had prepared me for. I was trained to be the hero, the one managing the show from center stage. Bruce hired me to be a hero maker, the one developing people for meaningful contribution. I came to Clear Creek to make my ministry dreams come true. But the people of Clear Creek were trying to make Jesus's dreams come true.

I would not appreciate the value of this awakening until years later. What happened that day shaped my paradigm of church ministry. I had experienced dynamic disciple-making relationships for over a decade in my late teens and early twenties. During those years disciple-making relationships were always more important than the programs that I attended. Relationship was always the main thing, and programs were just an excuse for the main thing to happen.

But at the onset of my first pastoral assignment I was tempted to make the program the main thing. The conversation with Dan was a blessed whiplash back to what I already knew. From day one as a local church pastor, God converted me to see people development,

> Relationship was always the main thing, and programs were just an excuse for the main thing to happen.

not program management, as job one. I wanted my life to equip the saints for ministry when my new title threatened to excuse them from ministry.

One expression of this paradigm shift was how I later designed small groups when I became Clear Creek's pastor of spiritual formation. At the time, we ran home-based small groups as our primary disciple-making vehicle. Yet in every training we reinforced the idea that groups existed to facilitate more intimate groups of three or four that focused on five practices of devotion to Christ. Every group leader training guide had three file tabs for them to write in the names of three people that they were investing in more deeply. A successful group meeting was not an end in itself but a step toward more important outcomes that could only happen in nonprogrammed relationships.

Dallas Willard articulated the point simply and concisely: "Spiritual formation doesn't happen in a program at the church. It happens by living your life. We really need to stay away from creating programs as our goal. Programs have their place, but they must be subordinated to the spiritual life."[1] Ray Ortlund echoes him: "We're not here to generate programs. It can be kind of self-validating and have an appearance of self-importance. Busyness can be equated with importance, but that's just not the way things go in the kingdom of God."[2]

Every Pastor's Daily Decision

My backstory reveals an important fork in the road of my vocational ministry journey. To this day I feel a great sense of susceptibility and vulnerability when I reflect on it. Beneath my conscious awareness I had two very different ministry paradigms before me. The automatic pilot of my internal navigation was directing me down the less biblical path of the program professional. I was on the verge of betraying all the best lessons I had learned from my previous ministry experience while I was still an amateur. I'm still amazed that I needed a minicrisis on my first day of postseminary, full-time ministry to jolt me onto a different path. I tremble a little when I wonder what would have happened to me if Dan *had* stepped aside to let me manage the children's ministry directly.

Fifteen years later, from a much different vantage point, I got a powerful glimpse of what I might have become. It was one of the most emotional moments of group facilitation I have ever led. I had the privilege of working with a group of pastors who were a part of a "leading edge" group of the one hundred largest United Methodist churches in the country. A bishop asked me to facilitate a learning group with twelve of these pastors in his annual conference. In our third session, there was no dry eye in the house even though these were all alpha male, senior pastor types.

What started the chain reaction of unexpected tears? The pastors grieved what they had lost in their success. One after the other, each pastor reflected on his call to ministry and his desire to make a difference through relational discipleship. Then each one painted the contrast between his early intention and his current role description at the helm of a booming church. They all found themselves managing ministry machinery they had never really signed up for.

Here's the real tragedy: in that soul-full afternoon we reflected, we shared stories, and we found a deep moment of true comfort together. But after a little weeping, each one went right back to his busy church schedule.

That could have been me. The crisis of Dan's phone call years earlier was a gift from God. It was a warning shot across the bow of my ministry ship. Would I devote my time, effort, and energy to the narrow way of relational disciple making or to the wide road of program management?

Maybe you have faced a similar fork in the road yourself. It's an investment decision and a directional decision that every pastor must make every day.

These experiences help us appreciate the personal dimension of the three kinds of churches we will explore in this chapter and through the rest of this book. To suggest that your church fits 100 percent into one of three molds may seem unfair and even polarizing. I understand that. But the longer and harder you look at the church across North America, the more these three churches emerge, and they will only become more clearly visible over the next twenty years.

The Three Kinds of Churches

We can see the three kinds of churches through the lens of the Upper Room–Lower Room paradigm. The picture-tool delivers value at three angles of view. At the narrowest angle, it helps you interpret your own ministry journey. A bit wider, it helps your local church to make disciples effectively. And at the widest angle it helps you understand the present moment and where the church at large is headed.

After twenty years of consulting, I am convinced that we are entering a twenty-year window that will witness the transformation of the church in North America. There is a vast and still multiplying number of ways to describe the church in our place and day, but I maintain that the best way to classify it over the next two decades is with this threefold formulation.

Type #1: Program Church—Organization without Disciple Making

In the first kind of church, leaders conceive of church growth and discipleship solely in terms of the LowerRoom. This church is big on organization but small on genuine, biblical disciple making. This is Church As We Know It; I call it *Program Church*.

I am not declaring that programs are bad in and of themselves or suggesting that the church should not have programs. I am simply naming the reality where attention on programs has become such a strong operational focus that a vision for and a culture of disciple making are eclipsed. Robust relational development is lost, because the programs have become an end in themselves.

My friend and longtime church consultant George Bullard has his own clever picture-tool to portray the problem of Program Church. George says that every church has four basic elements: *vision*, *relationships*, *programs*, and *management*. He sketches these as four people riding in an SUV (with a cross as the hood ornament).

In the healthiest, biblically functioning church, Vision is in the driver's seat, and Relationships sits in the front passenger position helping to navigate. Vision is George's way of talking about the Upper Room; Relationships represents the church's culture and practice of making disciples. Meanwhile, Programs sits in the back seat behind Relationships to support it, and Management rides behind Vision to help it drive.

In George's terms, Program Church emerges when Vision gets tired of driving and needs to take a nap in the back seat. When Vision pulls the car over, Management eagerly volunteers to drive. But Management wants his seatmate Programs to navigate, so

Relationships heads to the back seat too. The result is the un-healthiest seating arrangement in a church: Management driving, Programs navigating, and Vision and Relationships fast asleep in the back seat. Worst of all, no matter how tired Management gets, he hates giving up the driver's seat, and he demands that Programs keep sitting next to him! Even when Vision wakes up, it takes a huge effort to pry Management's fingers off the wheel.[3]

That is Program Church in theory, but what does it look like in real-life terms? Look around and you will find thirty-one Baskin-Robbins varieties of it. It is everywhere, whether your preference is traditional vanilla or the latest and greatest version of rocky road. Church leaders of every stripe have mastered Program Church. What makes Program Church isn't the style of the worship services or the presence or absence of a steeple. It's the attention of the leadership: in Program Church over 80 percent of the pastoral staff's energy is focused on running weekend worship and supporting events.

Many Program Church pastors feel uneasy about it the same way the previously mentioned Methodist pastors did. But just like those pastors, many have apparently succeeded with it. As I will recount in later chapters, Program Church quite simply worked for many years. People showed up; money rolled in. In many congregations, Program Church was so evidently successful that it seemed like madness to disrupt it. Attendance was booming and small groups were proliferating; surely the Lord's work was being done. Why rock the boat?

> In Program Church over 80 percent of the pastoral staff's energy is focused on running weekend worship and supporting events.

But all the while something was missing, and in their spirits many pastors and other attenders could sense it. Now, however, more people are noticing Program Church's increasingly obvious impotence.

From 2015 to 2020 the most gifted and talented leaders in every faith tribe—even those hailed as successful according to prevailing opinion—experienced the crisis of attendance frequency decline. Put another way, not even the most "excellent" and "relevant" programming (to quote the era's buzzwords) has stopped regular attenders from attending less frequently. That doesn't even count the landslide of the nonreligious in emerging generations who are not attending anywhere at all. (There are most certainly exceptions to the rule of attendance decline, which I will address in later chapters. For now, suffice it to say that I question whether their growth has been generated from disciple-making gusto rather than celebrity magnetism and staged spectacle.)

But the current crisis may also be an opportunity. It is becoming increasingly difficult for Program Church to validate itself by touting consistent worship attendance and sustainable budgeting. Coasting along is no longer an option—the time is up. In the hearts of many, from leaders to attenders, holy discontent has awoken. People are hungering and thirsting for a better way to do church than the Lower Room.

Type #2: House Church—Disciple Making without Organization

The second kind of church rejects the Lower Room altogether and endeavors to operate solely from the Upper Room. Proponents of this form of church believe (at least implicitly) that Church As We Know It is irredeemable—that it is so distorted by generations of disciple faking, which has warped the demands of attenders and bent the assumptions of leaders, that it is impractical or even impossible to fix it from the inside. This church exists as unincorporated relational networks meeting in relatively small groups in homes and public spaces. It is small on organization but big on disciple making, and it is commonly known as *House Church*.

House Church is also known as "microchurch," "organic church," or "simple church" (not to be confused with the book *Simple Church*, by Thom Rainer and Eric Geiger).[4] Despite my label "House Church," which some House Church practitioners dislike,[5] this church may meet anywhere that people get together. The number of participants gathered in one place is small and relationships are intimate. Leadership is shared widely and is not professionalized. Yet these are also characteristics of a small group in Program Church. House Church is different because participants consider the group itself to be church, not a program of a church. It has no features of organized, institutional Christianity as we are familiar with it—that is, no Lower Room. More importantly, the church does not consist in its meeting but in its web of life-on-life, disciple-making relationships, and it is constantly looking to reproduce new simple churches. To adapt George Bullard's analogy, House Church is a two-seat roadster with Vision driving and Relationships riding shotgun. It is all Upper Room.

I recently met Shawn, an ex-pastor of small groups who got so fed up with his role description that he resigned from his north Dallas–based megachurch with five thousand weekly attenders. He now does construction work for his income, but making disciples is his passion and continues to guide his calling. The day we talked, Shawn had been leading a House Church for about eighteen months and had twenty-six people in his family room for worship. With a vibrant glow, he celebrated with me how a handful of people had come to Christ in his neighborhood since he started meeting. What I appreciated most about Shawn was his joy. He wasn't mad at the organizational expression of church; he just realized that he didn't want to invest his life in that model any longer.

Brad, on the other hand, was a little less joyful as he pondered the frustration of organized church. A few years ago, this college buddy of mine moved to San Antonio and asked me to recommend some churches to him. Two years later, we got together for coffee. "How's everything going at church?" I asked.

"Not good," he replied, revealing his profound discouragement. "I love Jesus and I love his people," he said, "but I am not sure if it's worth going every Sunday to hear the talk and watch the gig." The way he described his home-based small group gripped me the most. "It's like we inject the church program into our home," he said. "We talk about community, but that's not what we experience. A few weeks ago, it came to a head for me when a couple in our group announced they were getting a divorce. We had been 'doing life together' for over a year, but no one in our group had a clue what was going on." He reported it all with a look of bewildered disbelief.

Six months ago, Brad broke out of the organized expression of church for the first time since he became a deeply committed Jesus follower. When I asked what he named the new group he started, he smirked: "G.O.P.G.—Group of People Gathered." You could hear the disdain in his voice for anything too official sounding.

These two House Church cameos represent a broad movement that I will not be discussing in this book. I want to clarify that while I am not a House Church practitioner myself, I do have a great respect for those who are. From living room chats with my friend Neil Cole to vigorous conversations with Frank Viola, I have rubbed shoulders with simple church thought leaders over the years. (If you are interested in learning more about making an intentional journey into missional communities, I recommend the resources and coaching of Alex Absalom, who with his wife, Hannah, leads Dandelion Resourcing, which equips churches to develop missional disciple-making cultures.)

Before leaving the topic of House Church, it is important to note that this is not a fad or something that is insignificant right now but might happen down the road. A 2009 study by the Barna Group revealed that anywhere from 4 to 33 percent of American adults claimed they had attended a House Church in the past month—the reason for the wide variance being the different ways the question was asked. Nevertheless, fully 10 percent of respondents said they had "attended a worship service in someone's home, known as a house church" within the past month.[6] Church leaders who don't get a steady diet of simple church content may not be aware of how prominent the movement is. It is fairly invisible compared to the industry of the organized church, but it is not going away.

Type #3: Future Church—Organized Disciple Making

By contrast with both Program Church and House Church, the third kind of church operates with both a Lower Room and an Upper Room. It maintains the place, personalities, programs, and people of the Lower Room, and it strives to make them accessible and excellent. Yet it entirely subordinates the Lower Room to the Upper Room's disciple-making vision; in other words, the institutional church serves relational disciple making as Jesus modeled, taught, and commanded. This church does not choose between organization and disciple making; it practices "organized disciple making." I call it *Future Church*.

Leaders in Future Church follow the practical strategy Dallas Willard proposed to the institutional church almost a quarter century ago: "We are, of course, *not* talking about eliminating nondisciple, consumer Christianity. . . . But we are talking about making it secondary, as far as our intentions are concerned. We would intend to make disciples and let converts 'happen,' rather than intending to make converts and letting disciples 'happen.'"[7]

A more recent voice describing Future Church is Brian Sanders. His exodus from Program Church was marked by the passion and longing of my House Church friends Shawn and Brad:

> When I first started talking about "leaving the church" . . . I argued it was the structures that needed to be left behind in order to build something better, something closer to our convictions. . . . I never told anyone to leave the church; I told people to leave the structures and programs that masquerade as church. I told people to leave the church of their deep frustration in order to take their place in the true and enduring church.

Yet as Sanders lays out his process of rethinking church and eventually launching The UNDERGROUND in the Tampa Bay area, he describes what I have always wanted church leaders to gain through the Vision Framing process. Sanders's new kind of church did not leave organization altogether but rather reinvented it:

> The UNDERGROUND started with no obligations and no expectations other than orthodoxy and our integrity. We ended up with something more similar to traditional church than I ever would have imagined. We take offerings, sing songs, gather on Sundays, preach sermons, ordain elders, and meet in a building. But to us, these elements are different because of how we use them, and now that we've worked through each of them for ourselves, we own them. We came to decisions about these practices as free people. We carry these traditions forward because we have come to see that God is in them, not because of what was done before or will be done again. We have taken the church to pieces and, little by little, have rebuilt a form that we love.[8]

This is the sort of church that I am advocating for. I want to clarify early on, however, that I am not making a statement against House Church even though I believe that Future Church is the greater opportunity for the local church in North America over the next twenty years. The term "Future Church" is not meant as a critique of House Church, because I am sincerely excited that the House Church is flourishing. Rather, Future Church is a counterposition against Program Church to show it for what it is: a counterfeit of the real thing.

I also do not employ the term "Future Church" to claim that organized disciple making is a new thing. Quite the opposite: for two thousand years, every church and movement with a public presence that has made genuine, multiplying disciples through the gospel has been Future Church. Rather, I name this model Future

Church as a proclamation of hope for the organized church for the next twenty years.

Bringing Batman Back to the Church

The bulk of this book is devoted to describing Future Church, where both the Upper Room and the Lower Room are going strong, so I will not detail it further quite yet. Instead, I want you to feel the angst and the energy of young church leaders who are passionately longing for something more.

It has been a long time in coming. The last twenty years we have witnessed a missional reorientation that has at last reached a generational tipping point in church leadership. As I will describe

Figure 2 – Three Kinds of Churches

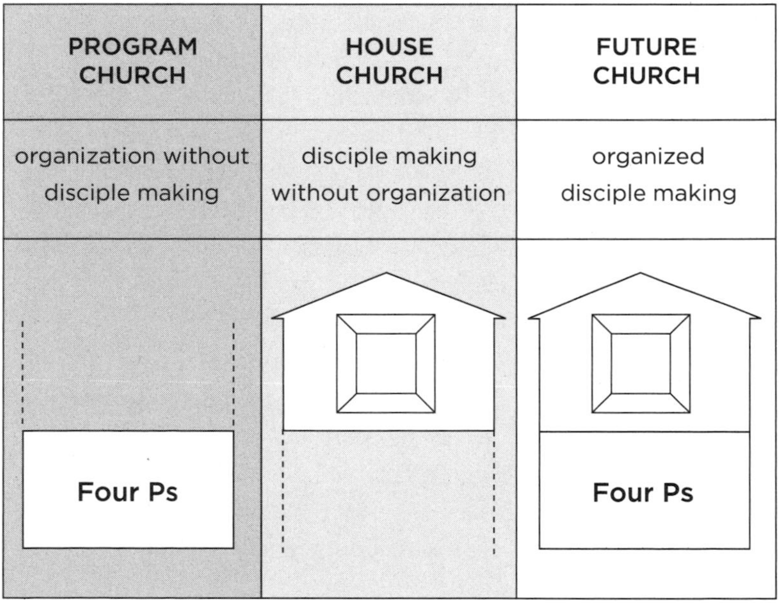

PROGRAM CHURCH	HOUSE CHURCH	FUTURE CHURCH
organization without disciple making	disciple making without organization	organized disciple making
Four Ps		Four Ps

later in this book, the missional paradigm and the expectation of disciple making that began to be introduced around the year 2000 have finally begun changing the priorities of leaders at every life stage. But the zeal for missional disciple making is especially strong among younger ones (ages twenty-one to thirty-five) who are spearheading it in action today with new, deep conviction.

I have two sons in their twenties, both of whom are in full-time church leadership. Our conversations keep me bracingly aware of how ministry looks from the point of view of a young leader. One of them told me about his friend and colleague Braden, and I couldn't stop thinking about something specific he said.

"All day long as I'm working at my church, I feel like Bruce Wayne," Braden said. "That's the person the rest of the staff and the church people see. Then a few nights a week I spend time talking about Jesus with unbelieving friends where we hang out, and I get to be Batman. Some of these guys are coming to Christ and I'm discipling them, but it is totally disconnected from what I do in ministry for a paycheck.

"I don't want to be two people anymore," Braden continued. "I want to be Batman all the time—even in my church."

This is the heart cry of a generation. Like every reader of this book, they heard a call from God and have given their lives to serve him. But they can't abide doing it in Program Church anymore, and increasingly they won't. So the question facing all church leaders is this: what does it take to allow Batman—Braden, yes, but also you—to come into the light?

The only way is for leaders to discover the Upper Room, climb up, and start living and leading from it. You might be raring to go already. But before we can explore the Upper Room's dimensions, we have to uncover the forces that keep leaders stuck in the Lower Room. Paraphrasing Alvin Toffler, we have to unlearn before we can relearn.[9] For until we deliberately decode and unlearn the ways of Program Church, we are doomed to scramble fruitlessly to maintain it.

OFF MISSION

What Keeps Leaders Serving a Functional
Mission That's Not the Great Commission

At some time or another, someone commissioned you into ministry. You might recall your graduation from Bible college or seminary, an installation ceremony at your first church, your ordination, or maybe just the handshake that said, "You have the job."

The commission you received probably echoed Scripture. Someone might have said, "Preach the word" (2 Tim. 4:2). Maybe someone said, "Be strong and courageous" (Josh. 1:9). Very likely someone quoted the Great Commission—"go and make disciples" (Matt. 28:19)—but even if not, it was probably in the atmosphere. In any case, at the outset you likely heard something that articulated a clear if open-ended mission.

Then you got into your actual job, and one of the most difficult things about it was knowing whether or not you were succeeding in that commission you received. Amid the blizzard of responsibilities and occasional cloudbursts of criticism, how did you know you were getting anywhere? What scorecard could you look at to know you were succeeding? How could you know you were getting results?

Two Kinds of Results

One of our challenges when we start out in ministry is grappling with a job where results aren't obvious. Yet when we gain more experience, the trouble is recognizing different kinds of results for what they are. Not all ministry results tell the same story or have the same value.

I articulated this concept in my book *Innovating Discipleship*, where I compared *input results* with *output results*.[1] At first those terms may be a little confusing, because the term "input results" might sound self-contradictory (like a square circle) and "output results" might sound redundant. But there is an important reality lying behind these terms.

Church leaders conventionally measure worship attendance and giving, commonly styled "nickels and noses," "butts and bucks," and "Attendance, Buildings, and Cash (the ABCs)." Leaders generally consider numbers of people and amounts of money to be outcomes of ministry activity; in other words, the bodies and the money that came in today are the result of what we did yesterday.

There is truth to this view, but it is also misleading. People and money are properly outcomes only if the goal is to get more people to show up and more money to come in. But this is not the goal of the Great Commission. Jesus never said, "Go into all the world and get people to show up—and if you have a healthy bottom line, I'll be pleased with that too." The actual Great Commission is to make disciples. If disciple making is our task, then people and money are not outcomes but *inputs*.

Inputs are the things that churches put into the front end of the ministry machine. People who come into contact with the church are the raw material (so to speak) for the disciple-making process; they are what the church has to work on. Money also goes in the front end; it is a catalytic ingredient added to the ministry process in the form of paid staff, curriculum, a building, and so forth. People and money, then, are input results.

So, if people and money are input results of a church's disciple-making process, what are its output results—what comes out the other end of the ministry machine? Put another way, all the activity of the church ultimately produces . . . what?

This is a question that most leaders never ask, much less answer, despite its enormous importance. Each church should look at itself to see what its activity is actually producing. What God wants it to produce is named most succinctly by Paul in Colossians 1:28—to present every person "complete in Christ" (NASB).

We can break that imposing output result down further, however. For example, a church could define its intended output results as the triad of faith, hope, and love (1 Cor. 13:13) or the ninefold fruit of the Spirit (Gal. 5:22–23) or the eight Beatitudes of Jesus (Matt. 5:3–10). We could even scour the Bible for descriptions of Christlikeness and build a custom list. In fact, I routinely encourage churches to do this very thing in order to express the measures of Christlikeness in a way that fits their particular context.

Even so, such a list of discipleship outputs is still too lofty and abstract. Abstract qualities like joy and purity of heart always retreat in leaders' minds before the concrete measurables of attendance and cash. The trick is to convert spiritual qualities into marks that a person can more easily observe.

For example, one attribute of perfection in Christ is genuine love for other believers. If we're operating according to the common functional Great Commission—"make more worship attenders, baptizing them in the name of small groups and teaching them to volunteer a few hours a month"—we would likely measure love for others by whether the person regularly attends a small group. But a better way to measure it is by whether the person has a *2 a.m. friend*, a friend they could call at two o'clock in the morning with a problem and that friend would drop everything to help, and vice versa.

Is a 2 a.m. friend a perfect measure? No, but it is much better than mere participation. It encapsulates a genuine ministry output, a real result of what our churches should be doing in people's lives as they are formed as disciples of Jesus who obey everything he commanded. It is the kind of thing you think about if your primary attachment is to the church's Upper Room.

> Where your measure is, there will your heart be also.

This illustration is only an introduction to the topic of ministry measures, which is beyond the scope of this book. The point here is that what we measure is intimately entwined with the mission we are really about. *Where your measure is, there will your heart be also.*

Unfortunately, the hearts of church leaders are under enormous pressures to dwell on input results over output results. These input results threaten to entomb their hearts in the Lower Room.

Under Pressure from Input Results

Pressure #1: Input Results Are Visible and Countable

Paul wrote that "we fix our eyes not on what is seen, but on what is unseen" (2 Cor. 4:18) and that "we live by faith, not by sight" (2 Cor. 5:7). Yet that is not easy to do! Our human minds are built so that we cannot help but put weight on what we apprehend with our five senses, especially what we see. For this reason, input results are impossible to ignore.

When you walk into the worship space on Sunday, you cannot help but see and silently measure how full the room is with people. In fact, you don't just see it, you *feel* it. Sight combines with sound, touch, and even smell to give you a sense that there is a buzz in the air—or not. When it is present, it can be intoxicating; when it is missing, it can be depressing.

In addition, input results are the easiest thing to measure, and their numerical data is as crisp and clean as they come—blessedly black and white. It does not take a particle accelerator to count heads; it does not take an electron microscope to read an account balance. While it may take intuition and expertise to interpret the data's meaning, it takes nothing but counting and adding to get the raw numbers.

Pressure #2: Input Results Are Legitimate Output Results in For-Profit Business

People and money—which ought to be considered input results in the church world—are output results in the business world. Increasing customers and revenue are goals that all businesses have in common. This business viewpoint strongly influences many churches.

Many of the lay leaders in churches—especially the ones with the most influence—are also leaders in the business world. They spend all day working to maximize customers and revenue, so it is entirely natural for them to bring that mindset with them as they drive through rush-hour traffic straight from the office to the church board meeting.

In addition, because people and money are indeed essential to keep any organization running, it is easy for them to serve as the low-hanging fruit of success, especially in times of fatigue or stress. When I was in college, I remember thinking sometimes, "It doesn't matter how I spend my time, as long as my grades are good." Even as a church consultant, during some trying times I've just been happy that the bills are getting paid. Likewise, it is common to have a shared, unspoken feeling in a church that whatever else might be going on, if people and money keep coming in, we're "all good."

Pressure #3: Input Results Are Symbols of Success

Attendance and giving are the practical standard for how proficient a leader is. In my work with Denominee, I routinely lead teams made up of pastors from very different sized churches. I was recently in a meeting with pastors leading churches of 50, 250, 550, and 3,500—a rare group in Christian circles because larger-church pastors are usually unlikely to collaborate with pastors of smaller ones. The question commonly asked (or at least silently thought) when pastors get together—"What's your weekend worship attendance?" or simply "How big is your church?"—isn't just to get an idea of what another pastor's ministry situation is like; it's regularly the measuring stick of the pastor's leadership ability and vocational success.

> Worship attendance is still the most reliable way to be regarded as an elite performer in professional ministry.

This doesn't just happen on a collegial level but on a national level. *Outreach Magazine* is famous for its lists of the one hundred largest and one hundred fastest-growing churches in America with the senior pastor meticulously noted in the description of each. To its credit, the magazine has recently added a list of one hundred reproducing churches. But we have yet to see a magazine publish a list of the one hundred most prayerful churches in America or the one hundred churches that have commissioned the most full-time cross-cultural missionaries. In North America today, worship attendance is still the most reliable way to be regarded as an elite performer in professional ministry.

Pressure #4: Input Results Justify Higher Pay

Dave Rhodes, cofounder of Younique, notes that the wider the gap is between what an average church participant is competent to do and what the senior leader is competent to do, the more unique and special the leader appears. Then the more special the leader looks, the more money the leader might be able to make.

For example, if a leader is able to grip the attention of two thousand people with skilled communication, and none of those two thousand people is able to do the same, the leader demonstrates high value to the church and has the potential to command a higher salary than they would otherwise. As a result, it is in the leader's personal financial interest to attract more people to their own stellar performance and persuade people to help keep it going.

But note that this is the opposite of how disciple making works. Jesus talked about training students to be like their teacher, and he promised that those who believed in him would do even greater things than he did (cf. Luke 6:40; John 14:12). Jesus's ironic ambition as the unique Son of God was to make himself as un-unique as possible. That ambition would cost him in today's church.

Whether a leader is influenced by love of money varies from person to person and is not the main issue. The point is that the paycheck, which is meant to free the pastor to do God's work, can also become a subtle, biweekly reinforcement and reward for being special, for doing things that other believers cannot, which is directly related to the number of people who show up to watch the leader do it.

Pressure #5: Input Results Maintain the Social Contract

In a voluntary society where no one is compelled by some authority or intense peer pressure to attend church, people go to a church because they like it. Consequently, every stable or growing church rests on an unspoken social contract between participants and leadership: participants expect the leaders to deliver the things they like, and leaders expect participants to keep participating.

There are probably some people in your church who like for you to challenge them from the Word of God to grow in Christ and provide practical training for them to do so. Yet there are probably also people in your church who like for you to provide a positive weekly experience of moving music and uplifting preaching, a fun and wholesome environment for their kids, perhaps a pleasant circle of just-close-enough friends, and maybe a vehicle for them to do their hobby in a setting that looks like service. They secretly hope that even their minuscule commitments to church stuff will still register as good enough.

Now consider the temptation this poses for church leaders. Whether they know it or not, these participants want their spiritual success defined as mere attendance. *That is the very same definition of professional success that the pastor is pressured to adopt* for all the reasons we have outlined so far. So it is the easiest thing in the world for the pastor to set the bar low, because then everyone clears it, including him- or herself. Participants stick around and even more come, soothed by justification by attendance. Meanwhile, the pastor's leadership is applauded due to validation by numbers. Everybody wins.

Energy Follows Attention

With all these pressures and temptations bearing down on pastors, is it any wonder when input results become our fixation? Is it any surprise when we doggedly pursue ministry success in the Lower Room? It would be stranger if we did not. Yet the long-term consequences are devastating. In John S. Dickerson's searing words:

> Whatever you focus on, that person or problem will get your energy. . . . We have been so attentive to numbers, among other things . . . that we have not focused on genuine relational discipleship. This is not because we think discipleship is unimportant. Any Christian leader will tell you it is . . . of undeniable, utmost importance. But examine the calendar, the weekly routine of us pastors and leaders, and you won't find much room for relational discipleship. . . . The "tyranny of the urgent" has overtaken us. The late-20th-century church model, in many applications, requires so much energy and attention that little to nothing is left for anything else, including discipleship.[2]

As Dave Rhodes observes, New Testament believers would never have conceived that a person could be a leader in the church without being held responsible to make disciples. But today, with all the Lower Room responsibilities that Program Church loads on leaders, it is not only possible but probable that your church's leaders, from the video person to the lead pastor, are not individually making disciples but rather hoping that somehow the team as a whole is getting it done.

Dickerson concludes that "the late-20th-century church model, in many applications, requires so much energy and attention that little to nothing is left for anything else, including discipleship." His remark about "the late-20th-century church model" alludes to yet another pressure on leaders to labor at the functional Great Commission: the pressure of history. None of us emerged into ministry from nowhere; we were formed by generations of structures, assumptions, and teaching about what church growth is all about. Therefore, we cannot step forward into Future Church until we learn our past.

SIXTY YEARS

*How Twentieth-Century Church Growth
Influences Twenty-First-Century Leaders*

When I started serving a church fresh out of seminary in the 1990s, I was attracted to the best church-for-the-unchurched models. But around the year 2000, not long before I began working with churches as a consultant, I started catching the currents and winds of an emerging gulf stream—new thinking about church and the mission of Jesus. Twenty years have passed since then, and we currently live in a time of unprecedented complexity regarding church methodology. For the first time in two decades, I believe we are ripe for another paradigm shift that is now in the making. In fact, *Future Church* means to reframe that shift.

My mentor Len Sweet was the first to model for me up close the reality that a great futurist will always be a great historian. He uses an analogy from golf: to hit the ball farther you need a deeper backswing. Similarly, a church consultant's work sometimes resembles that of an archaeologist. When I get to know a church, I dig through layers of ministry sediment consisting of programs, structures, and philosophies laid down by leaders and influences of earlier eras. What every church does today is the product of the layers already laid down with contemporary ministry ideas sitting on top. Many older churches have as many as four ministry paradigms influencing today's activities despite the incoherence of the different philosophies.

As I have gotten to know the geological layers of North American church ministry, I have concluded that a church growth model becomes increasingly pervasive over twenty years before it peaks and begins to be overtaken by a new one.

From 1940 to 2020, then, there have been four generational waves of how to do church. We might think of these as eras of church growth, each a response to the social circumstances of its time and also often a reaction to the ministry model that came before it. This book predicts the paradigm of the next twenty years, and therefore it describes a full century of church growth eras—the eighty years behind us and the twenty years still ahead.

> From 1940 to 2020, there have been four generational waves of how to do church.

For the moment we will tour the first three eras, which extend from about 1940 to 2000. Keep in mind that dates are approximate. There are always churches that exemplify an era before I say it begins and after I say it ends. Also note that I display the models and the differences between them in high contrast to make them easier to recognize even though many churches were never pure examples of just one paradigm. Caveats aside, the purpose of our tour is to show how generations of twentieth-century assumptions still pressure twenty-first-century leaders to define success by the input results of the Lower Room.

The Wartime Revival (1940–1960)

In 1940, multiple challenges stressed Protestant churches in the United States. In addition to the national crises of economic depression and a spreading, global war, fundamentalists were still licking their wounds from losing denominational institutions and cultural influence to liberals in the church and the academy in the 1920s, and they were still huddling behind circled wagons in their religious tribe.[1]

But a national religious revival began during World War II that generated enormous church growth. The uplift in church attendance became most pronounced during the early years of the Cold War. The growth came from two sources that were neither precisely inside nor outside the church. In this era, church growth came from *beside* the church, the interface between congregations and wider movements.

One of the growth engines was the work of an emerging generation of fundamentalists who wanted to reenter and influence American society again. They wanted to hold to orthodox doctrinal convictions, but they were tired of playing defense and sought to reengage the nation with the gospel and biblical truth. Some were intellectuals and institution builders who labored to replace the structures lost to liberals in the previous generation.[2] But others were a band of evangelists who captured young people's attention under the banner of Youth for Christ (YFC).

These evangelists gave the Anglo-American revivalist tradition a facelift and found eager audiences. In 1943, they began filling arenas with teenagers looking for something to do in their cities amid the gasoline rationing of the war. Soon thousands were making commitments to Christ. After the war, YFC preachers expanded their appeal to a broader audience, and the movement went supernova when William Randolph Hearst's newspapers began publicizing the 1949 Los Angeles tent meeting of YFC evangelist Billy Graham.

The other growth engine of the wartime revival was the looming threat of global communism following World War II, intensified by the danger of nuclear annihilation. Americans increasingly saw their country not only as the guardian of democracy and liberty against totalitarianism but also as the godly opponent of "godless communism" (a common slogan of the day), a link that Graham himself implicitly encouraged in his preaching. The term "Judeo-Christian" was coined to fold previously marginalized Catholics and Jews into the Protestant nation as a united front. "Under God" was added to the Pledge of Allegiance; "In God we trust" was made the national motto. Americans broadly agreed with then-president-elect Dwight D. Eisenhower's remark: "Our form of government has no sense unless it is founded in a deeply felt religious faith, and I don't care what it is . . . but it must be a religion with all men created equal."[3]

The church came to be seen again as a highly important community institution, a rallying point for upstanding citizens, and therefore a place to see and be seen. During the Eisenhower administration, as many as four out of five Americans attended a worship service on a given weekend, the highest mark in American history. As a community institution, however, the church was often indistinguishable from the exploding number of fraternal, charitable, and youth organizations, all of which gathered doers of good and were sanctified by ritual prayer at their orderly meetings.

Growth in the wartime revival came from next door to the church—from the parachurch and civil religion. The church's job was to be a stalwart, soul-saving, morals-inculcating, nation-supporting pillar of the local community alongside others. The individual Christian's job was to be a godly community member and attend revival meetings featuring traveling evangelists, forming the "studio audience" for the spectacle in which sinners in attendance might be saved. Between genuine awakening by the Spirit of God and patriotic anxieties, churches did not have to do much to grow in the 1940s and '50s besides unlock the door on Sunday morning.

The Golden Era of Denominationalism (1960–1980)

By the time Eisenhower yielded the White House to John F. Kennedy in 1961, the wartime revival was losing steam. National unity was beginning to be torn apart over segregation and civil rights and soon by Vietnam, the sexual revolution, feminism, and a devastating loss of faith in the trustworthiness of institutions. New Age religion would eventually present Americans with spiritual options far outside the Judeo-Christian mainstream.

But the church did not know this at first. The problem it saw in 1960 was not a social or cultural problem but a demographic problem—and an opportunity.

The baby boom was in full swing, and home construction also boomed in the suburbs sprouting up around North American cities. Each denomination realized that if it did not erect buildings and plant congregations in the new communities, another denomination would—or no one would. In response, denominations set up franchises to suit churched people's religious preferences in suburban growth areas.

The church-planting initiatives of the 1960s and '70s often had less to do with disciple making than with math. I once consulted with a United Methodist church in a Houston suburb that began growing explosively in the late 1970s. As I got to know the church, I watched a video that gave the pitch for why the church needed to be founded. Methodist brass knew that the community would grow by x residents in the ensuing years and that y percent of the new townspeople would be Methodists. Therefore, a church had to be founded to accommodate them. The church's job was to put door hangers at the homes of new residents to catch immigrating Methodists and perhaps draw in a few others.

I recently talked to a Southern Baptist denominational leader in Ohio who described the church growth of his era

> The church-planting initiatives of the 1960s and '70s often had less to do with disciple making than with math.

as "grits evangelism." Evidently southern pastors attempting to start a church in the north would wait and watch for people to pick up a box of grits in the supermarket aisle. Then they would introduce themselves as the pastor of a new Southern Baptist church in town in hopes of winning new congregants.

There were few established community organizations in new suburbs, so the church responded by becoming a full-service community organization itself, a place where something was on the calendar for some member of the family every day of the week, catering to every need and interest. There was a program for everyone, from a choir to a softball team to Alcoholics Anonymous to a women's Bible study while the kids were in school to a men's breakfast on Saturday morning. New church constructions featured Christian education wings that resembled new elementary schools, and Sunday school became the relational connecting point for children and adults alike.

The church growth lessons of the golden era of denominationalism were first "if you build it, they will come" and second "a church for the whole family." The result was a programming philosophy that more is more. If a church had the volunteer force to staff a program and the money to build a facility for it, people would join the church to access it.

The New Permission Era (1980–2000)

The suburban church-planting strategy was in touch with the residential construction trends of its time, but it ignored the staggering cultural shifts of the Sixties (so-called; the period actually spanned from about 1963 to about 1974). By 1980, it was no longer safe to assume that people were looking to attend a church of the denomination in which they were raised. More seriously, it could not be assumed that people were looking to attend church at all, even though the vast majority had a church background.

Emerging leaders began to grapple seriously with the problem of reaching millions of lost, dechurched baby boomers and their families. Some—most prominently Rick Warren in Orange County, California, and Bill Hybels in suburban Chicago—attempted to go back to the drawing board, discard the church paradigms they knew, and design a relevant experience from the ground up that would draw lost people to Christ.

The church was to be built for the outsider, not the insider; everything was reimagined from the perspective of the "seeker," a fairly new term in the ministry dictionary that rapidly rose in prominence. Formal was out and casual was in. The sound of worship and flow of the service were entirely converted to new forms springing from the soft-rock/folk songs of the 1970s Jesus Movement. Sermons started from the practical felt needs of semi-secular people and ended with biblical counsel rather than proceeding from the reading of a biblical text. The welcome of visitors—soon to be termed "guests"—was transformed by influence from the hospitality industry. Everything in the church ran on outstanding customer service.

The shift of the new permission era was in one respect the aftershock of a titanic economic shift that gathered momentum earlier in the century. According to Brian Sanders,

> Futurist Paul Saffo argues that the industrial manufacturing complex was born on the impulse to overcome scarcity at the turn of the last century. The result is what he calls a "producer economy"— the hero of which was the manufacturer. Eventually these factories became so efficient that they were able to not only overcome scarcity, but to overproduce. As we created and accumulated more than we needed, consumption became the primary impulse. This new era gave us what we all recognize as a "consumer economy," whose hero was the marketer, the one who could convince us to want what they were selling.[4]

Whereas the golden era of denominationalism was driven to mass-produce more churches and more programs for them to run, the new permission era was driven to market the faith to oversold, convenience-sensitive consumers.

There were dozens of easy-to-spot differences between a new permission church and a church built in an earlier era operating down the road. But the greatest difference was much deeper than drums versus organ or khakis versus suit, even deeper than home groups versus Sunday school; the new permission church saw itself as solely responsible to reach the lost for Christ. It did not expect any help from parachurch organizations, itinerant revivalists, civil religion, cultural Christianity, or denominational heritage. It functioned on the conviction that the local church was the only organization God put on earth to save people who disliked or dismissed what they thought they knew about the Christian faith.

Every aspect of the new permission church was built for this goal. Rick Warren asserted that a biblical church has five purposes, but the outline and page count of his book *The Purpose-Driven Church* gave away that evangelism was the prime purpose of Saddleback Community Church.[5]

Nevertheless, evangelism in the new permission church was conditioned by its organizational assumptions. New permission churches, especially the pioneering ones, talked about both the come-and-see and go-and-tell aspects of evangelism.[6] It was Bill Hybels, after all, who taught believers to "just walk across the room" to an unsaved acquaintance.[7] But the vast bulk of time, effort, energy, and manpower in the new permission church was devoted to perfecting the come-and-see part. Even go-and-tell personal evangelism shifted from "come to Jesus" to "come to my church." The mature church member was expected to extend invitations to a weekend seeker service where the platform speaker would offer salvation.

Because of its organizational bias, the discipleship model in the new permission church was the assimilation funnel. The term "assimilation" itself reveals that the objective of discipleship was to make newcomers *similar* to others in the organization. The journey of growth in Christ was aligned with steps in a process of organizational participation from worship services to small groups to volunteer service. Growth, then, was measured by the number of participants in each program in the process. The goal was to move people into the core—the church's committed labor force and donor base—as the climax of Christian maturity. Growth in character was strongly desired and sincerely taught, but attendance, contributions, and volunteer hours were what counted because they *could* be counted. (We will explore the new permission assimilation funnel in greater depth in part 3.)

Three Generations of Assumptions

To repeat, churches pick up features of all the eras they pass through. Then they pass those features on to us leaders who were formed in the churches. We go on to serve churches that harbor these assumptions and that expect us to abide by them.

Table 1 - Three Eras of Church Growth, 1940-2000

	Wartime Revival (1940-1960)	Golden Era of Denominationalism (1960-1980)	New Permission Era (1980-2000)
Church Identity	Teaching center with promotion of national ideals as a community institution	Teaching center with doctrinal legitimacy and membership in a familiar faith family	Teaching center with applicable truth and ministry involvement at church
Ministry Philosophy	More is more	More is more	Less is more
Attraction Driver	Prominent option	Heritage option	Relevant option
Rally Cry	We are the best church in town	We are the best church in the tribe	We are the best church for the times
Evangelism Paradigm	Disciple as audience	Disciple as representative	Disciple as inviter
Worship Promise	Provide unity	Provide liturgy	Provide relevance
Connection Vehicle	Fraternal organization	Sunday school	Small group
Retention Method	Community service	Full service	Customer service
Maturity Model	Christian citizen	Program activity	Assimilation funnel

So what are some of the assumptions about growth that churches have absorbed over the years?

- Church growth is secured by individual commitments made in a decision at a public event.
- Church growth results in the church being a visible and prominent community institution.
- Church growth comes from providing programs that young families want to access.
- Church growth requires a culturally relevant and inspiring public experience with outstanding customer service and hospitality for the audience.
- Church growth is measured by the numbers of people attending and serving in worship services and other programs arranged as steps in a linear process.
- Above all, church growth has to do with what organizations do, not what individuals do, except insofar as individuals support the work of the organization.

All these assumptions silently pressure leaders to gauge their effectiveness in Christ's mission by body count—the number of people who show up at the organization's public events and the size of the building required to accommodate them. These assumptions pressure leaders to devote their energies to maintaining and improving the Lower Room. In addition, they pressure leaders to confuse assimilation with biblical disciple making.

I have more to say on the topic of measurement in part 2, but we are not done looking at what keeps leaders off mission just yet. Since churches and leaders crave church growth, an industry exists to meet that need. Unfortunately, the industry's most popular prescriptions for growth keep churches stuck in the Lower Room while real church growth remains elusive.

ATTENDANCE UPPERS

Three Pills Prescribed by Church Pharma

At the close of the previous chapter, I referred to an industry that exists to meet churches' and leaders' felt need for church growth. It is also worth mentioning, if it is not already evident, that I am part of that industry. The fact that you (or someone) paid to pick up a book called *Future Church: 7 Laws of Real Church Growth* makes that obvious all by itself.

We could call this field of enterprise the church-industrial complex. I also like to call it *Church Pharma*, an industry that produces and sells therapies to fix churches' health and growth problems.

I am happy to serve the church through Church Pharma. I've spent most of my professional life serving the Lord in this vein, and over that time—including today—I've had a hand in every industrial sector that I reference in this chapter. There is nothing I enjoy more than assisting churches in the mission God gave them, and I have found God calling me to do so in this field.

Yet there is a shadow side to Church Pharma. Think of it as the helping-selling dilemma.

Helping and selling are not opposites. To the contrary, every organization that genuinely resources the church—whether for-profit or nonprofit—must both help the church and sell to it. An organization must help the church in order to be justifiable, but it must successfully sell to the church to be viable. If a resource purveyor isn't justifiable, it *shouldn't* last; if it isn't viable, it *won't* last. So, every legitimate organization serving the church wants to offer resources that both help and sell.

But a temptation lurks here. The helping-selling dilemma is this: *Do we offer what we know will help at the risk that it might not sell, or do we offer what we know will sell at the risk that it might not help?*

The trap is that it is much easier and quicker to know if a product sells than if it helps. In addition, the organization feels much more acute and immediate pain if a product doesn't sell than if it doesn't help. As a result, a good deal more pressure bears on the selling side than on the helping side. There is a great yet subtle temptation to call a sale a win even if it doesn't really help the people who bought the product.

> It is much easier and quicker to know if a product sells than if it helps.

Church leaders also feel pressure—especially pressure for the church to grow—so they feel a need for help in many areas. Busy leaders tend to be attracted to done-for-you resources, and they have been conditioned by the market to expect them. For these reasons, it does not take a complicated formula to make money trying to help the church.

For example, the largest consulting industry in the church since the 1960s has been capital campaign consulting, which is usually about investing in place in the Lower Room. This industry is sustained by the felt need of raising money for a church's building project coupled with the fear of loss and the promise of gain around fundraising.

A newer industry is church staff search—especially for churches with five hundred or more in attendance—which has grown rapidly over the last decade. The first felt need that drives talent search is the fear of losing momentum when there is no lead pastor or key ministry staff in place; churches scramble to rebuild the personality factor of the Lower Room when it disappears. Another felt need is tied to program: because of the relentless urgency to keep Program Church afloat every Sunday, it is necessary to find talent fast to keep it going. Either way, hope is extended that somebody outside the system can come and maintain or grow the system.

Christian publishing is a much longer-established sector of Church Pharma. It caters to leaders' FOMO (fear of missing out) on the latest and greatest ministry ideas. The industry responds to the need by distributing the books of superstar pastors who are believed to have the answers. But it sells even more books when the book itself is the answer—that is, when a book is the heart of a campaign with an accompanying sermon series and discussion guide that promises to ramp up attendance or small group participation for an out-of-the-box numerical win.

Content marketing is a newer sort of publishing industry that has become its own sector of Church Pharma, but it also extends the other sectors at the same time. Online content aggregators meet the felt need for a convenient, no-cost, one-stop shop of successful techniques and keeping-up-with-the-Joneses comparisons with other churches. The content sector makes it easier for those who sell best to sell most, but it does not necessarily enable those who *help* most to sell most.

Taken as a whole, these felt-needs-driven industries are large and lucrative. The more these services profit, the more capital they have to invest in growing their product line and extending their marketing. Organizations get better, stronger, and faster at selling products, but their products almost universally fix a leader's focus on the Lower Room.

I do not mean to insinuate that the organizations of Church Pharma are primarily motivated by profit over a desire to build up the church. Rather, I am saying that profitability is easily taken as a proxy for real help to the church, and profit also accelerates how much more the organization can sell. The organizations and industries that I am talking about do not sell bad things. It's just that the things they sell rarely address, much less solve, the church's overwhelming and supremely important challenge: how to move from faking disciples to making disciples.

> An organization's products almost universally fix a leader's focus on the Lower Room.

In this chapter we look at some of the stuff that Church Pharma sells church leaders to cure what ails them. These growth pills—the elixir of engagement, the medicine of multiplication, and the placebo of pastor change—are actively peddled and eagerly swallowed. Leaders take them because they promise to get their numbers up.

Engagement, multiplication, and pastor change—each of them does indeed have a legitimate definition, location, and function. When churches and their leaders are operating on a two-level floor plan with an Upper Room and a Lower Room, all of these are beneficial and even essential. But when the Upper Room is empty, these pills become something different than they were meant to be, and they exacerbate the Lower Room fixation of Program Church.

The Elixir of Engagement

In chapter 3, when I described how a church gets off mission, I observed that leaders habitually look at worship attendance as their primary or even sole measure of accomplishment. That said, most church leaders in North America these days aren't looking at that figure because it pumps them up. To the contrary, it weighs them down.

As I noted earlier, attendance figures are on the decline in churches of all kinds. Even churches that expect to grow each

year and are rarely disappointed have stumbled onto an attendance plateau. This is partly because the church struggles to dem-
onstrate the relevance, value, and necessity of in-person church
attendance to emerging generations of nonreligious people and
even to believers. Yet it is also because attendance frequency
is on the decline; in other words, regular attenders attend less
often.

All church leaders recognize this phenomenon at some level,
and the topic has gained traction in ministry literature over the
past several years. In 2013 Thom Rainer called decreasing attendance frequency the number one reason for attendance decline.[1]
My post on declining attendance frequency was the most read
on my blog in 2015.[2] In the same year, five months after Carey
Nieuwhof's podcast debuted, Nieuwhof interviewed me on that
subject, and the topic reappeared as a chapter in his book *Lasting
Impact*.[3]

Yet just because church leaders recognize that frequency decline has an effect on attendance doesn't mean they have quanti-
fied how significant the effect is. Let's say your committed attenders used to come to worship 3.2 times per month on average,
but now they come 1.7 times per month (both reasonable estimates, though figures vary from church to church). The impact
of the frequency decrease on your average weekly attendance is
dramatic (see table 2).

Church growth is hard enough to come by, but it is even harder
when you are rowing against the current of attendance decline. In
this tidal shift, a church has to surge forward just to stand still—it
has to grow just to maintain. Some churches are experiencing what
I call "growteauing": their number of regular worshipers is increasing while weekly worship attendance remains flat. Growteauing
can be discovered and validated through careful measurement
and statistical analysis, but a telltale sign is when attendance at a
church's special events (such as Easter) increases year upon year
but attendance on ordinary weeks stays the same.

Table 2 – Effect of Decline in Attendance Frequency at Different Congregational Sizes

Number of Regular Worshipers	Past Average Worship Attendance Minus Guests (estimated 3.2x/mo)	Current Average Worship Attendance Minus Guests (estimated 1.7x/mo)
100	74	39
250	185	98
500	369	196
1,000	738	392
1,500	1,108	588
2,500	1,846	981
5,000	3,692	1,962
10,000	7,385	3,923
15,000	11,077	5,885

Average worship attendance is equal to the number of weeks of attendance per regular worshiper per month, times the number of regular worshipers, times 12 months per year, divided by 52 weeks per year.

This makes for a very troubling time to be a church leader, especially if your functional Great Commission exalts worship attendance as its first and foremost metric. Yet there is more than one way to respond to the crisis. One approach is to consider why Program Church has lost value in people's eyes and to reimagine what it means to be the people of God biblically in a community. This is the approach I intend to take in this book.

But there is another approach advocated by some prominent voices. It is summed up in the phrase "engagement is the new attendance." As the argument goes, mere attendance was never Jesus's objective; he wanted people who were all in. We are now at a cultural moment in which casual Christians, mere attenders who are not all in, are no longer coming to church. The future of the church belongs to the highly involved and the seekers, who are really the people the church ought to consist of anyway (and did in the first century). These engaged people will in turn drive attendance.[4]

I agree with 100 percent of this. The rub, however, comes at this question: What does "engagement" mean?

The default way to define engagement is participation in parts of the church program other than worship—most notably small group attendance, volunteerism, and giving. If a person is doing these things, they can be said to be engaged. A church can count even more people as engaged if it includes streaming views or attendance at a virtual campus. If you tinker with the numbers long enough, you can often find a formula that provides some good news about how engagement is going strong.

Don't misunderstand me. I want all believers to engage in intimate groups of believers, in service to others, and in giving. These are all good and necessary activities for every follower of Jesus. And I am delighted when any true seeker encounters the gospel online. The problem is that these things still make for an inferior definition of engagement. Recalling the ministry machine metaphor from chapter 3, this just replaces tallying inputs with counting *throughputs*; that is, instead of adding up how many bodies go into the front end of the ministry machine (worship services), we are merely measuring how far people make it through the bowels of the machine (other programs). We still are not measuring outputs—actual changes in the life of a disciple of Jesus Christ.

Focusing on this kind of engagement is not a cure; it is a painkiller. It is an incremental response, not a qualitative response; it treats symptoms instead of promoting health. It helps leaders feel better about their declining results by changing the scorecard; measuring online attendance, small group attendance, volunteerism, and giving makes the drop in Sunday worship attendance feel less painful. But it does not compel leaders to reinvent the church's value proposition for a new era in line with a biblical model of mission. It continues to seek validation from attendance at Lower Room programs, not from the impact of Upper Room disciple making *through* Lower Room programs.

The Medicine of Multiplication

A second pill that churches take to boost their attendance figure is *multiplication*—birthing new fellowships and worship gatherings in new places. As with the engagement activities described above, I am totally on board with multiplication; I believe it is essential and biblically faithful for a church to multiply. However, as with engagement, multiplication as commonly practiced can obscure a church's disciple-making reality and stymie, not stimulate, its development.

At the congregational level, perhaps the most popular manifestation of multiplication is *multisite*. My best attempt at a definition of multisite is a single congregation that originally gathered for public worship in one location but now gathers in multiple locations, yet it still considers itself a single congregation under one name and unified leadership.[5]

The first North American multisite churches may have come into being as early as the 1980s, but the breakthrough year was 1998. That year North Coast Church in Vista, California, began using video to broadcast the sermon to other locations on its campus. As video and communications technology evolved, it allowed North Coast to multiply locations off campus as well.[6] Community Christian Church in Chicagoland hit upon the same solution at about the same time, and other churches followed soon after. Leadership Network reported the existence of five thousand multisite churches in 2012 and a figure of eight thousand two years later.[7] Current estimates range as high as fifteen thousand churches.

There are several good reasons for a church to go multisite. If a church's Lower Room programs are pistons in a true Upper Room disciple-making engine, going multisite can leverage the church's reputation for excellent quality to disciple more people. The drive to multiply sites also reminds members that the church exists for those who are not yet a part of it, so it fosters a missional mindset. Multisite churches take a great deal of people power to pull off, so they tend to activate a greater proportion of the congregation in service. This also raises senior leaders' awareness of their need for a leadership development pipeline and spurs them to take initial steps in developing one. In addition, going multisite may also be a move closer to local context, putting church where the people are and styling it in the way that is most suitable to them. (On the other hand, some multisite churches adopt the franchise model of identical venues, often amplified by a broadcast that elevates a single teacher's platform over local leaders, which is less sensitive to local context.)

In many cases, however, these are not the reasons that churches have taken the multisite route; they are merely side benefits. The main reason churches have gone multisite is simply to get bigger.

The generic, default, unexamined vision most commonly found in churches—especially churches less than thirty years old that have not peaked in their life cycle yet—can be summed up in one word: *more*. More people, more attenders, more volunteers, more staff, more reach—and now, more sites. With more as the motive, church leaders have found multisite to be a cheaper way to build a bigger box, which was often the thing they were really hoping for.

> With more as the motive, church leaders have found multisite to be a cheaper way to build a bigger box.

Ironically, multisite started as the bubble-gum-and-duct-tape solution to the problem of having more people coming than could fit into the building. Now, twenty years later, multisite is sold as a well-packaged solution to the problem of growth stagnation. Rather than going multisite to accommodate those who already want to attend, churches are using it to try to persuade more people to attend, with uneven results.

When multisite does not arise naturally from multiplying disciples, leaders, groups, and worship services, it is merely an extension of the Lower Room. The key determiner is whether reproducing disciples is viewed as the cause or as the effect of launching a new site. For example, one multisite consultant insists that the reason for going multisite is not to get a bigger church; rather, it "is about obeying the Great Commission to make disciples who make disciples who start churches that start churches." He continues, "After the launch of a new multisite congregation, the key to retainability, sustainability and growth is doing the basics of discipleship and outreach in the community with the good news and good works of the gospel."[8] While these statements are true at face value, they also betray an assumption that multisite expansion is the basis for a new wave of disciple making rather than the other way around.

Unfortunately, the typical site launch requires so much energy to create a new funnel for attendance inputs that it saps strength from producing discipleship outputs. Leaders can unconsciously sink into a strategy that says, "We'll get a big church first, then we'll disciple the people who come." But in the endless drive for the next one hundred people, actual disciple making stays on the back burner. In this scenario, multisite becomes a medication to increase a church's apparent virility, not nutrition to increase its potency.

I know pastors who, in my discernment, should not be pushing their church in a multisite direction. Instead, they should focus their church's energies on being renewed around disciple making. But these pastors are clinging with white knuckles to their need to add numbers, and multisite appears to them as the tried and true way to make it happen. As a result, they build additions onto the Lower Room instead of a staircase to the Upper Room.

But the problem with multiplication not only manifests in multisite; it can also appear in church planting. I have always been and always will be passionate about church planting, so I cannot believe that a day would come that I would say this. Yet over the last twenty years, I have seen that church planting can appear to be disciple making when it actually is not. Three anecdotes illustrate the trend.

First, every year I coach at least a dozen church planters in the prelaunch phase of their plants. My role is to help them achieve clarity on a contextually appropriate vision before the church is born. The planters I work with are almost always young; as with any emerging generation, their perspectives are a mixture of openness to new ideas and an uncritical reflection—unable to conceive of an alternative—of what they have experienced in their formative years.

Over time working with these groups, I have encountered a consistent fifty-fifty split. Half of the church planters are making disciples who will become churches; the other half are planting programs. When I hear the planters articulate their disciple-making strategies, half are planting disciples and hoping for churches to come; the other half are planting churches and hoping for disciples to come.

My second anecdote further reveals how we multiply Program Churches while assuming we are making disciples. I was talking with the staff of a prominent church with a reputation for church planting whose pastor is a well-known advocate of sending. This church is good at raising up and sending professional church planters, but the pastors admitted to me, "We don't have anything for the soccer mom; we're not sending her." To their credit, they commit considerable resources to multiplying organizations and sending willing workers to support them, but when it comes to the granular level of sending and multiplying individual disciples, they are at a loss about what to do.

The third story comes from the most uncomfortable initial church interview I have ever experienced as a consultant, which came about while I was penning these pages.

The second-chair pastor had invited me to his church, describing disunity among the staff; the senior pastor believed the church's vision was crystal clear, but others on staff disagreed. That was all I knew about the church, but the situation is not uncommon. My approach was not uncommon either; I began our meeting by asking the same question I ask every church in every condition: "What is your greatest growth challenge?" I began by listening to the answers of the less experienced staff members and gradually worked my way around the room. As the staff shared openly, however, I noticed the senior pastor becoming visibly frustrated.

When at last it was his turn, the pastor unloaded. He started by pushing back on my question by asking his staff, "Who told Will we have a growth challenge?" Unaware that I had merely asked a question that I ask every client, he was demonstratively defensive that anyone would imply his church was not growing. Then he dismissed the insinuation by insisting, "Our church's *total impact* is growing."

What evidence did the pastor give to support his rebuttal? He said the church had planted two churches in the past three years. That spoke volumes to me, because the contentious conversation I had with him and his staff does not happen when a church multiplies out of disciple making. Upper Room church planting does not rationalize an attendance plateau and make it uncomfortable for anyone to acknowledge reality as if it is an inadmissible, shameful secret. Healthy church planting is not a technique to put points on the board; it does not idolize attendance growth and then reproduce the idolatry in new churches and staffs. But that is what happens when church leaders reach for any Lower Room technique that promises to keep growth pointing up.

The Placebo of Pastor Change

As we have seen, church leaders are tempted to *simulate* growth by engagement in *programs*. They are also tempted to *stimulate* growth by multiplication into more attractive *places*. But churches also *seek* growth by upgrading their chief *personalities*: their senior, lead, or solo pastors.

It is tricky for a church to get and keep a pastor who will bring growth. On the one hand, a pastor needs to survive challenges early in their tenure and develop trust with the congregation before the best stuff comes out of the relationship after about the fourth year. On the other hand, at some point both pastor and church get a bit too comfortable, and unless the pastor significantly reinvents or reenvisions their ministry after fourteen years of tenure (which is rare), the church begins to coast. Unpleasant as it may be to admit, growth often stalls because the senior pastor has become so familiar to the people and also because he or she is simply getting older. For these reasons, the charisma-driven, Lower Room attractor of personality no longer delivers the way it used to.

Meanwhile, a tantalizing option waits in the wings: a new pastor. When growth stalls or never gets started under a pastor, churches can swap in a new pastor who embodies a new direction and then ride the wave of energy that surges in the early part of their tenure.

Churches that want to pump up growth with the perfect pastor have roughly the same person in mind: a thirty-three-year-old married father of 2.3 kids. This candidate happens to have the same specs as the new attender the church most wants to attract, the sort of person who is likely to make the biggest overall contribution to the church now and in the future.

Churches selling themselves to attenders upgrade their pastors the same way that homeowners putting their houses on the market upgrade their kitchens—they aim for the new style that's in vogue. Despite a church's godliest intentions, the natural groove is to seek a strapping King Saul to make them like the other nations and lead them to victory. They don't want much—only the best. I know one ministerial staffing professional who quips, "Every church wants Jesus riding a unicorn."

Without a doubt, good pastoral leadership is critically important for a church's growth, and fortunately there are many gifted leaders out there. But getting a new pastor is often a Lower Room placebo. It does not actually improve the body's disciple-making health; it merely gives the body the appearance of recovery because the patient expects it to work. I don't mean to diminish the genuine seeds that a pastor can sow for a bountiful discipleship harvest in a church in the first two years of ministry, but they take time to develop. The typical honeymoon surge in attendance is not the fruit of a new pastor's strong disciple-making leadership but rather personality-driven novelty.

Can You Trust the Paradigm?

The three pills we have looked at in this chapter are only a portion of Church Pharma's whole medicine cabinet. For example, one popular book details systems to "drive growth" in churches, yet growth is entirely defined as getting more people into the big room on the weekend. If you search the work for specific terms, you will find "church" five hundred times, "grow" eighty-one times, and "attend" forty-nine times. Yet if you search for "disciple," "discipleship," or "disciple making," you will not find them at all. I have no problem with solid insights and techniques for a particular aspect of building a great Lower Room. The problem is confusing that one part with the whole of real church growth.

Here is another example. I haven't touched on one of Church Pharma's most popular therapies: the remedy of revitalization. Against the backdrop of the epidemic stagnation and decline of small and long-established churches, a cottage industry has boomed to provide solutions for pastors in these ministry settings. But the wholesome and necessary prescriptions written by revitalization experts—biblical teaching, good leadership, organizational health, spiritual growth, local outreach, even prayer—do not get at the root cause of decline in these churches. They do not suffi-ciently grapple with the oppositional forces churches are facing today that were not so strong even twenty years ago. And they do not adequately point pastors and churches to the Upper Room.

Revitalization didn't work in Cory Hartman's churches the way experts predicted. Read his story at futurechurchbook.com/bonus.

All the interventions of Church Pharma described in this chap-ter remind me of something Professor John Hannah said during my seminary days. When telling and interpreting stories from church history, he often said, "They did the wrong things for the right reasons."

Over my years as a consultant, I have witnessed this feature of human nature many times. When I sense that a client is rais-ing their defenses in the face of an uncomfortable reality, I often respond, "I trust your heart; I just don't trust your paradigm." A person can have the healthiest heart in the world, but if their eyesight is bad, they are still liable to miss a turn and take the wrong road.

This could be said both about Church Pharma and about the thousands of faithful church leaders who buy what it sells. I trust their hearts' intent but not the paradigm by which problems are defined and solved. I do not trust a paradigm that appears to be ig-norant of the Upper Room, that confuses it with the Lower Room, or that promises Upper Room results out of Lower Room hustle. I do not trust a paradigm that appeals to pastors who want to make disciples but only keeps their churches faking disciples.

It's past time for a different paradigm.

INTERLUDE

The Missional Reorientation

I n chapter 4 I traced the evolution of church growth from about 1940 to 2000. The rest of this book describes the fundamental principles of Future Church, which I believe will prevail over the next twenty years. Before we explore the era to come, however, we must bridge the gap by briefly touring the period from 2000 to 2020, a time that I call the *missional reorientation*.

Around the year 2000, some vocal thinkers began sharply critiquing the church paradigms of earlier eras, including the new permission era. They did not stop at the recent past either; indeed, it was not unusual for them to criticize standard modes of doing church going all the way back to the Roman emperor Constantine in the fourth century. These thinkers were sometimes painted with a broad brush as "emergent," a fuzzy label that was coming into vogue at the time, but it soon became apparent that many of them had different concerns than the leading lights of that camp. Instead, the term that became most associated with their school of thought was "missional."

The missional perspective brought a significant paradigm shift from the new permission era while still promoting an outward-facing posture for God's people. Both new permission ministry leaders and missional thinkers believed that God ordained the local church to reach the world with the gospel. Evangelism and missions could not be delegated to a parachurch organization, a traveling show, or secular structures that encouraged faith. They were the church's job.

Yet the missional movement followed that belief to a more radical place than new permission ever dreamed of going. Although new permission churches owned the importance of evangelism, they did so with a focus on methodology, not identity. In the new permission era, church leaders designed churches that the unchurched would love to attend. Their playbook involved drawing people to and revolving them around a central church location, a pattern that was as old as the late Roman Empire.

Missional thinkers, by contrast, pushed the conversation to recalibrate the very identity of God's people. The point wasn't to have a church with a missions department but to have a missional church. The focus on the church's identity flows out of an understanding of God's identity as a God on mission. The Great Commission of this era is John 20:21: "As the Father has sent me, I am sending you." The goal is to see each person as an everyday missionary, living sent where they live, work, and play.

> The focus on the church's identity flows out of an understanding of God's identity as a God on mission.

Naturally, then, everything missional stresses the church scattered as a counterbalance to the church gathered. Church is not where you go for a few hours each week but who you are 24/7. Missional proponents made provocative statements like, "It is not so much that the church of God has a mission as the mission of God has a church."[1] They sought to transform the imaginations of Christ followers to see themselves as the church on the move and to see the gathered experience as a secondary function of believers' primary identity. As the new permission era reflected the shift from a producer economy to a consumer economy, the missional reorientation anticipated a shift to a creator economy, one that revolves around the individual as producer instead of the organization as producer.[2]

By reimagining church, missional thinkers fundamentally challenged the soundness of the new permission assimilation funnel. Yet because the mental shift the missional reorientation required was so elemental and so contrary to how church leaders had been formed, this era of church growth thinking differed from all that came before. Unlike previous eras, no predominant lived-out model emerged for others to imitate. The missional paradigm, therefore, became a provocative and powerful emphasis that gave birth to various expressions and hybrid models. Many experimented, piloted, and dabbled. But it did not fundamentally change the face of the church over two decades of influence the way previous paradigms had.

It did change leaders' minds, however. Many pastors in this era, especially young leaders entering ministry, were shaped by missional concepts and examined the church they inherited through missional lenses. For this reason, I call this era the missional reorientation. Unlike the introductions of previous church growth paradigms, this one did not take place in ministry settings but in the minds of leaders who, fueled by holy discontent, looked for ways to put it into practice.

Missional ministry appeared in embryo in a variety of loosely connected streams. Unlike previous movements, it arguably did not begin in the United States—at least not solely—but in Great Britain and nations of the Commonwealth; an intellectual ancestor of the movement was British missionary Lesslie Newbigin. The first American church organizations to show interest were not in the evangelical orbit but among theological moderates in the Protestant mainline who invited presentations from thinkers like Australians Alan Hirsch and Michael Frost and Canadian Alan Roxburgh. This initial intellectual embrace in the mainline rarely became practical, but missional concepts began establishing an organizational footprint among evangelicals with networks like

Forge, The Missional Network, Verge, and an organization that I started with Alan Hirsch, Neil Cole, Dave Rhodes, and Jessie Cruikshank called 100 Movements. It also exerted influence on conference platforms like Future Travelers, Presbyterian Global Fellowship, Sentralized, and Exponential.

Missional thinking was applied in Upper Room–only form in organic churches (i.e., House Church), as led and described by Neil Cole and others. Meanwhile, other strategists worked to put the public, organized church on a missional footing. Mike Breen pioneered missional disciple making in England and brought its principles to the United States through 3DMovements (3DM), consulting with churches to form missional–new permission hybrids. Acts 29 sought to plant missional churches with a forceful, Reformed Baptist character. Meanwhile, Tim Keller had quietly been formulating a missional theological vision and "middleware" for churches in cosmopolitan megacities, eventually launching an international church-planting initiative, Redeemer City to City.

It is impossible to list everyone involved in the missional church conversation. In addition, my purpose is not to tell a comprehensive story but to position what I call Future Church in the context of what has come before. My intention is for Future Church to synthesize the insights and priorities of the missional reorientation and apply them to the institutional church. Future Church approves and continues to amplify the missional character of hybrid churches in the first decades of the twenty-first century. This is only possible because, over a twenty-year span, missional principles have changed the minds of a critical mass of church leaders who want more than the church is currently producing.

The Seven Laws

The foundational propositions of Future Church are expressed as seven laws. These encapsulate the principles of organized disciple

Table 3 – Five Eras of Church Growth, 1940–2040

	Wartime Revival (1940-1960)	Golden Era of Denominationalism (1960-1980)	New Permission Era (1980-2000)	Missional Reorientation (2000-2020)	Future Church (2020-2040)
Church Identity	Teaching center with promotion of national ideals as a community institution	Teaching center with doctrinal legitimacy and membership in a familiar faith family	Teaching center with applicable truth and ministry involvement at church	Teaching center with mindset shift to be the church not just go to church	Training center where disciple making is expected of everyone
Ministry Philosophy	More is more	More is more	Less is more	Out is more	To be is more
Attraction Driver	Prominent option	Heritage option	Relevant option	Community option	Training option
Rally Cry	We are the best church in town	We are the best church in the tribe	We are the best church for the times	We are the best church for the city	We are the best church for your calling
Evangelism Paradigm	Disciple as audience	Disciple as representative	Disciple as inviter	Disciple as missionary	Disciple as reproducer
Worship Promise	Provide unity	Provide liturgy	Provide relevance	Provide encounter	Provide integration
Connection Vehicle	Fraternal organization	Sunday school	Small group	Missional community	Microgroup
Retention Method	Community service	Full service	Customer service	City service	Vocational service
Maturity Model	Christian citizen	Program activity	Assimilation funnel	Living sent	Multiplying practice

making, and they succinctly state what distinguishes real church growth:

- *The Law of Mission*: real church growth starts with a culture of mission, not worship.
- *The Law of Power*: real church growth is powered by the gospel, not relevance.
- *The Law of Love*: real church growth is validated by unity, not numbers.
- *The Law of Context*: real church growth is local, not imported.
- *The Law of Development*: real church growth is about growing people, not managing programs.
- *The Law of Leadership*: real church growth is led by calling, not celebrity.
- *The Law of Vision*: real church growth is energized by shared imagination, not shared preference.

These laws are more than simple steps or handy how-tos. Rather, they are principles that must forge our conviction and then our practice or else the best church growth tactics in the world will devolve into faking disciples.

These Seven Laws of the Upper Room, therefore, start with the heart. They challenge the leader to first ask, "What is really happening in my church today?" I have aimed in part 1 to reveal the gnarly strength of the Lower Room paradigm. The wording of each law contrasts a Lower Room reality—worship, relevance, numbers, importation, programs, celebrity, and preference—to an Upper Room possibility. Like the law of gravity, I don't see these as opinions but as the true science of the Spirit that is acting on us every day. If you choose to ignore them, you can stay the course with Program Church and cling to an illusion. If you choose to embrace them, they just might warm your heart and kindle new courage. You just might fall in love with ministry again.

As you wrestle with each law, they will illuminate a pathway that is new yet familiar in a strangely spiritual sense. I hope the laws bring you hope in the wonderful Upper Room possibilities of mission, gospel, unity, localness, people, calling, and imagination. You were made to lead in and from the Upper Room!

Fittingly, the Seven Laws are arranged in parallel with what the medieval church called the Seven Virtues (see table 4). The first three laws correspond to the three theological virtues of 1 Corinthians 13:13: the Laws of Mission (hope), of Power (faith), and of Love. On that foundation I build four more laws that correspond to the four cardinal virtues of Greek philosophy—the Laws of Context (temperance), of Development (fortitude), of Leadership (justice), and of Vision (prudence). I know that at first glance the dots don't necessarily connect. But I think you will enjoy how this correlation cultivates interest and understanding as we dive into each law.

In part 1 we deconstructed Program Church to give us a clear space to build on. In part 2 we construct the Upper Room by exploring its Seven Laws one by one. For each, I attempt to establish

Table 4 – Seven Virtues and Seven Laws of the Upper Room

Virtue Sets	Seven Virtues	Seven Laws
Theological Virtues	Hope	The Law of Mission
	Faith	The Law of Power
	Love	The Law of Love
Cardinal Virtues	Temperance	The Law of Context
	Fortitude	The Law of Development
	Justice	The Law of Leadership
	Prudence	The Law of Vision

its biblical basis, contrast it with much of Church As We Know It, and give examples of how it plays out in real life.

Before we take actions, we establish convictions; there is no practical without principle. The next step for Future Church leaders, then, is to learn the rules of the Upper Room.

PART 2

MAKING DISCIPLES

THE SEVEN LAWS OF THE UPPER ROOM

THE LAW OF MISSION

Real Church Growth Starts with a Culture of Mission, Not Worship

I magine that you were being forced to go away from your church for a long time, and you did not know when you would ever be back. You might be battling a terrible disease. Or you might serve in a country with anti-Christian persecution and you could be thrown into prison at any moment. In any case, you are about to lose touch with your flock, and you want to prepare them for that.

You conclude that one part of preparing your people for your departure is to make a list of the most important truths to remember: the things you never, ever want them to forget, the first things that anyone new to the faith should get to know. This isn't a random thought experiment; it's been a common occurrence in the history of the church ever since Jesus gave his disciples important instructions just before he went away (John 14–17). So, if you had to leave a legacy in the form of a list, how would you kick it off? What is item number one? What principle at the top sets the tone for the whole and puts it all in perspective?

One group over 350 years ago started their list with this historic statement: "Man's chief end is to glorify God, and to enjoy him for ever."[1] That is an impressive thirteen words: contemplating them makes me feel like I'm on the top of a mountain on a cold, brilliant day, surveying the rocky, snowy majesty all around. "Man's chief end" . . . "glorifying God and enjoying him forever"—it is immense, sweeping, awe-inspiring. It is worship.

It makes sense to say that worship comes first, because God comes first, and God deserves to be worshiped, glorified, enjoyed forever. If I were writing a creed or a confession or a catechism, maybe I would start there too.

But when it comes to the Seven Laws of the Upper Room, I am not starting with worship. In fact, if I knew I would soon be unable to communicate with churches anymore and I could only share a short list of truths for them to remember, the very first thing I would want them to hear is that real church growth *does not* start with worship.

That might sound crazy, maybe even arrogant. God is awesome! Shouldn't any list of important truths for the church to remember start with how magnificent God is?

My reply is that we know how great God is by what he does. And what he does is pursue us on a mission to make us his own. He was on a mission when he made us and on a mission when he saved us. He sent Jesus on that mission, and Jesus sent his disciples on that mission. Someone told you and me about salvation in Jesus because they were on that mission. Now you and I are on the same mission today.

It's only because God was on a mission to win us for himself that we learned to worship him. It's only because he saved us that we praise him. In the same way, when we join the mission and live it out, worship always follows in its wake. In light of this truth, I propose the first law of the Upper Room: *real church growth starts with a culture of mission, not worship.*

Read more about how the Bible frames the relationship between God's mission and our worship at futurechurchbook.com/bonus.

When Worship Comes First

Every word in the Law of Mission is critical, but I direct your attention first to the word "starts." In organized disciple making, growth *starts* with a culture of mission, not worship. If you want worship, mission must take priority. That is where you have to begin. Because if you start with a culture of mission, you get worshipers. But if you start with a culture of worship, you get worship services. Between them lies all the difference in the world.

As I have already described, for a generation or more, church leaders have measured growth principally if not exclusively by the number of people who attend worship services. As I recounted in my book *Innovating Discipleship*, when I ask leaders how they want their church to be different in two years, I almost always get variations on two words: "more people," that is, higher attendance, especially at weekend worship.[2] In addition, the common church-planting model has rested heavily on if-you-build-it-they-will-come worship services.

> If you start with a culture of mission, you get worshipers. But if you start with a culture of worship, you get worship services.

The idea is, make worship services, get disciples; in other words, church growth starts with a culture of worship. Evidence that the worship service is central to a church's culture lies in the volume of financial, physical, and human resources it insatiably demands to keep going week after week. The more the worship service succeeds in amassing growth, the hungrier the worship machine gets and the more institutional wherewithal it sucks into its gravitational pull—especially when the pressure is on to make each weekend more spectacular than the one before.

Dave Rhodes and I have coached hundreds of new permission era churches, including more than a few megachurches and gigachurches. We always probe the question of how much time and energy goes into weekend service delivery. One time Dave queried one of the largest churches in the country, and the staff replied, "95 percent." That is not uncommon for a church of any size, but it is certainly amplified when you gather people by the thousands. Dave likes to pose the challenge, "If 80-plus percent of your church's time, energy, and effort goes into making Sunday morning happen, is it a church or a production company?"

The Unintended Messages of Worship Services

How can it be that a gathering to glorify God doesn't produce the disciple-making fruit that the worship service itself intends? How is it that worship for the purpose of mission can actually frustrate mission (and true worship as well)? It does so by communicating silent messages to participants that are much more powerful than the messages spoken in words.

The medieval church adopted a Latin motto: *Lex orandi, lex credendi*. Translated, it means, "The law of prayer is the law of belief." What the church regularly *does* when it gathers to worship and pray—before, during, and after anything is said—communicates more about what the church believes than what it *says* during the gathering. The *context* through which the church is communicating communicates more than the *content* itself.[3]

I would restate this idea today to say, "*How* you do worship services *somehow* informs everything else about following Jesus." We can compare the idea to Marshall McLuhan's famous phrase "the medium is the message." The nature of the worship environments that we draw people into (the medium) has an effect on their beliefs and actions (the message) that is far greater than the impact of what we tell them in that worship service.[4]

Different worship environments communicate different messages, to be sure; think of the different messages sent by a eucharistic mass with a ten-minute homily, a smoke-and-lasers rock concert with a twenty-minute pep talk, and a thirty-five-minute expositional sermon with an acoustic warmup. But there are certain unintended messages commonly sent by churches of every style that start with a culture of worship rather than a culture of mission:

- Church is a place you go to (versus a family on mission everywhere).
- Church is a part of your week/month/year (versus a family on mission every day).
- Church is a dispensary of services (versus a productive community).
- Worship is for inspiration and enjoyment (versus pleasing God).
- Ministry is for professionals (versus the opportunity of every believer).
- Service means activities that keep the organization running (versus actions that kindly help one's neighbor).
- An unbeliever's first point of contact with the church is the largest programmed event (versus their relationship with a believing friend outside church walls).

Every one of these messages reacts like static interference with what the Bible teaches, which is the very thing we are trying to convey in that worship service. These unintentional messages do not "equip the saints for the work of ministry" (Eph. 4:12 ESV); they may even excuse them from the work of ministry. We might preach the opposite of these messages, but the medium speaks louder than we do; while we are shouting we are really whispering.

There are indeed gatherings for worship in Future Church, but they send a different message because they start from a different place. Church planters leading from the Upper Room do not launch worship services to draw in disciples. Instead, they make disciples who worship. That is God's mission, and the Law of Mission means cultivating a community of mission as the starting point for real church growth.

How the Culture of Mission Began

Jesus was a man on a mission from God, but he did more than pursue the mission. Jesus recruited, trained, and sent apostles on a mission also, but his movement launched from a stronger base than those individuals. Rather, one of Jesus's greatest and most underappreciated accomplishments was to establish a *culture* of mission among his followers that perpetuated itself for generations. On the strength of the culture of mission that Jesus instilled in his disciples, his Way took over the Roman world and established itself in large portions of Africa and Asia in a few centuries.

Mission-driven individuals can be mighty, but they are short-lived. A culture of mission, on the other hand, has staying power; though it must be maintained and renewed in each generation, it has a way of keeping itself going long after the originators are gone. The only way to shape and keep a culture of mission in a church is with missional leadership. The supreme model for that is Jesus himself.

Jesus's Culture of Mission (Luke 6-9)

Our case study for how Jesus started with a culture of mission is Luke 6:12–9:56. These four chapters survey the experience of the Twelve from the time Jesus constituted them as a special team in Galilee to the beginning of Jesus's last journey to Jerusalem. The Twelve formed the core that Jesus was preparing to perpetuate the movement he started. The culture he would establish among these men would set the tone for the church for hundreds of years.

As Luke recounts it, after thirty years of personal mission preparation (1:1–4:13), two chapters concisely summarize what

Jesus's mission looked like for as much as two years: announcing the coming kingdom of God, teaching with authority, healing, casting out demons, hanging out with sinners, royally ticking people off (especially Pharisees), and calling people to follow him as disciples.

In Luke 6:12, Jesus chooses twelve disciples for an especially close relationship with him. He begins to establish the leadership culture immediately with the name he gives the group: "apostles." This English word is borrowed from the Greek term meaning "envoy." It is the official representative of an important person—in this case, the King—sent forth to speak on his behalf. Thus, mission is built into Jesus's team's language from the beginning. The top leaders in the Jesus movement are not rulers or governors or directors or managers. They are envoys, men without authority of their own who are sent on a mission with a message.

From observing and listening to Jesus as disciples, the Twelve had already learned about the kingdom of God, obedience, healing, sinners, forgiveness, opposition, and Jesus's unique and mysterious relationship to God. Now, as apostles, they relearn the same lessons, but the demands of Jesus's teaching are even more intense and his deeds even more dramatic than before.

Finally, in Luke 9 Jesus sends the apostles out in pairs to do what he has been modeling for them for months. Jesus states their mission succinctly: "he sent them out to proclaim the kingdom of God and to heal the sick" (v. 2). The apostles get the message, because they promptly go out "proclaiming the good news and healing people everywhere" (v. 6). When they get back, their debrief is interrupted by crowds thronging to Jesus, so he "spoke to them about the kingdom of God, and healed those who needed healing" (v. 11).

Is the mission clear enough? It is to *go, proclaim the kingdom,* and *heal.*

Then the Twelve learn new crucial lessons. Jesus moves from teaching the apostles the mandate of mission and the method of mission to the manner of mission. He explains that he is the Anointed One who will come in the glory of the Father and the holy angels. But he will submit to suffering and death—and resurrection—before that happens. Therefore, the model of greatness that he exemplifies consists in humble service and submission. Jesus even puts a little kid in front of the apostles' faces to illustrate the point. He also has to order the apostles not to interfere with an unknown stranger who is casting out demons in Jesus's name because that man is a partner in the mission too. All of this instruction reinforces and amplifies the culture of mission. The mission is all.

Culture of Mission Challenged (Luke 9:51–56)

The primacy of mission in Jesus's ministry is on display yet again in the episode that immediately follows. In Luke 9:51 Jesus says, in essence, "Okay, guys, you're as ready as you can be so far. Now we're going to Jerusalem so I can get killed." What the text actually says is, "When the days were approaching for His ascension . . . He resolutely set His face to go to Jerusalem" (NASB 1977). *He resolutely set his face*—is it possible to describe a missional attitude more vividly? Remember that Luke was a physician and knew the human body well. He uses and repeats this idiom twice in the passage. It is reminiscent of Isaiah 50:7, where the Suffering Servant says, "I have set my face like flint." The bottom line: When Jesus pivots to make a beeline to the cross, one could see mission in his disposition.

But there is a hiccup on the way to Jerusalem. Jesus sends messengers ahead to prepare a village of Samaritans to accommodate his group. (Again, Jesus is always establishing a culture of mission; he is always sending someone somewhere.) But the Samaritans, a minority marginalized by Jews, refuse to show hospitality to a Jew going to worship at Jerusalem. It is their defiant statement that their own temple on Mount Gerizim is superior. They are offended that Jesus will not validate the worship experience they have going on. It is as if Jesus is walking by the traditional worship service to go to the contemporary one, and the traditional worshipers are a bit hot under the collar.

For Jesus, mission trumps everything. And in this case Jesus's mission trumps the Samaritans' worship preferences. He is not self-important, but he is not nice either. He is not trying to attract a fan club, and he has no interest in pampering them with good customer service. Jesus was not about to express his love for the Samaritans in that village by accommodating them but by dying for them. So without argument he moves on to the next village. The mission remains supreme.

Unfortunately, while Jesus is riveted to his mission, his apostles James and John bust loose. Their egos are bruised and they blow their stack at the rude Samaritans. "Lord, do you want us to call fire down from heaven to destroy them?" they ask (Luke 9:54).

To review, the mission is to *go*, not to stop and fight with detractors. The mission is to *proclaim* the coming kingdom, not to bring a taste of the last judgment ahead of schedule. The mission is to *heal* people, not napalm them.

James and John know this, or they should. They have been watching Jesus for years, for some of the time at close range. His teaching has been explicit. How could they live with the Son of God for that long and think that torching this village is the right move?

The problem is mission drift. Mission clarity is not a checkbox; it is a commitment for life. It is not a mission statement; it is a mission state of mind. The all-time perfect leader spent years with his followers and was *still* developing a culture of mission among them. If Jesus needed to rebuke his disciples after that much time together, what makes any of us think we can do church and not continually clarify mission as the heart of discipleship? This story should explode our confidence in the mission fluency of our churches.

The Apostles' Culture of Mission (Acts 1–8)

With respect to mission methodology and context, the difference between Luke and Acts is something like the difference between parachurch and church. In Luke the mission is carried out by Jesus and his roving band of followers itinerating from city to city. In the first seven chapters of Acts, on the other hand, the mission is grounded in a particular locale (Jerusalem) and is carried out by an expanded family with many branches—a community of multigenerational families.

Despite those differences, however, the culture of mission that Jesus established among his disciples carried over to the new church family. The proof comes at the first crisis in the post-ascension mission, in Acts 6:1–6.

"The number of disciples was increasing" (v. 1), and the apostles faced their first serious growth challenge. They were accustomed to buying bread every day with believers' contributions and distributing it to poor widows whom the whole church family had adopted as their own. But the number of widows became too great, and some were being missed. Worse, the neglected widows were Greek-speakers—immigrants to Judea or pilgrims at Pentecost who never went home—which suggests bias on the part of the apostles, few of whom spoke Greek as their first language.

The apostles met the challenge by inviting the church to pick seven men to run the bread distribution. All of those chosen turned out to be Greek-speakers. Meanwhile, the apostles planned to concentrate their attention on "prayer and the ministry of the word" (v. 4).

When I talk through this passage with church leaders, I draw two boxes on a whiteboard, one marked "internal" and the other "external." I ask the leaders, "When you hear the phrase 'we will give our attention to prayer and the ministry of the word,' which box does that fall into?" They always pick the internal box, because they are thinking about preaching at worship services (for Christians) and prayer in small groups (consisting of Christians).

But how does the book of Acts define prayer and the ministry of the word? *As 100 percent external activities.*

The ministry of the word makes its first appearance when Peter preaches to the crowd at Pentecost and "three thousand were added to their number that day" (2:41). Just as in Jesus's ministry, the apostles' teaching was continually accompanied by "many wonders and signs" that filled everyone with awe (v. 43). An example is the lame man whom Peter heals in chapter 3. This healing led to another opportunity to proclaim Jesus to the onlookers. The apostles continued to perform miracles among "the people," that is, Jews in general, and they met in a section of the temple courts that was the largest and most trafficked area in Jerusalem (5:12). When the apostles were thrown in jail, an angel let them out and ordered them to "stand in the temple courts . . . and tell the people all about this new life" (v. 20). The greatest testimony to the external focus of the ministry of the word, however, comes from the Sanhedrin when they hauled the apostles back to court for a dressing down: "We gave you strict orders not to teach in this name. . . . Yet you have filled Jerusalem with your teaching" (v. 28). But that did not bother the apostles. "Day after day, in the temple courts and from house to house, they never stopped teaching and proclaiming the good news that Jesus is the Messiah" (v. 42).

What about prayer? After Jesus ascended into heaven, the believers prayed continually for ten days to receive power from the Holy Spirit in order to bear witness to Jesus to the ends of the earth (1:7, 14). Then the Spirit came, and they rushed into the streets to proclaim the kingdom in the languages of all the pilgrims to Jerusalem. They met to pray in the temple courts daily, "praising God and enjoying the favor of all the people. And the Lord added to their number daily those who were being saved" (2:47). Peter and John healed the lame man while they "were going up to the temple at the time of prayer" (3:1). After the Council rebuked them, they gathered the church together to pray. And what did they ask God for? To "enable your servants to speak your word with great boldness. Stretch out your hand to heal and perform signs and wonders through the name of your holy servant Jesus" (4:29–30). Then, "After they prayed, the place where they were meeting was shaken. And they were all filled with the Holy Spirit and spoke the word of God boldly" (4:31).

The conclusion is inescapable: prayer and the ministry of the word were not internally focused in the early church. To the contrary, they were the church's prime missional activities. So, when the apostles tell the church in Acts 6, "We will turn this responsibility [to distribute bread] over to them [the seven] and will give our attention to prayer and the ministry of the word" (6:3–4), they are saying, "We are going to delegate our internal activities in order to devote ourselves entirely to external activities." These men's priorities are now completely converted from the Lower Room to the Upper Room. When the church's top leadership is entirely occupied with going outward with the Word of God, you know the culture of mission is firmly established.

> Prayer and the ministry of the word were not internally focused in the early church.

Further proof is that the culture was not limited to the apostles but extended through the entire church. In Acts 8 the bulk of the church is scattered from Jerusalem because of persecution by Saul. The text is explicit that the apostles remained in the city, so it was only the rank and file who spread through Judea, Samaria, and beyond. But even these disciples "preached the word wherever they went" (v. 4).

Most illustrative are those who go to Samaria led by Philip, one of the seven bread distributors. Note that in Jerusalem the temple was both the mission space and the worship space for believers. The scattered believers have now lost both. So, which do they look to recover first—a place to worship or a place to do the mission?

As mentioned earlier, the Samaritans had their own temple on the top of a mountain. If worship were the believers' top priority, that is where you would expect to find them. But that is not where they went. Philip "went *down to a city* in Samaria and proclaimed the Messiah there" (8:5). The followers of the Way could be found with people who needed to hear the word. When they could no longer use the temple in Jerusalem, they replaced it with a new mission space rather than with a new worship space.

Redefining Hope

"And now these three remain: faith, hope, and love" (1 Cor. 13:13). Hope is easily neglected as the kid brother of the great virtues of faith and love, but this comes from a misunderstanding of biblical hope.

"Hope" is our unsatisfactory English approximation of the Greek word *elpis*. *Elpis* is not a wish or an insecure desire. It is an expectation of the future; it is what we believe is coming that shapes our behavior now.

When we are stuck in the church's Lower Room, our hope lies in the initiatives we take that we wish will bring in more people and make them happier. This temptation must always be resisted even in the Upper Room, where our vision may degenerate into what Dietrich Bonhoeffer called a "wish-dream" of what we want things to be like and how we expect to get them there.[5]

But the biblical hope that fueled the culture of mission of the apostles, the early church, and even Jesus himself—the hope that fuels the culture of mission for Future Church—is the hope of the coming kingdom, the last judgment, the resurrection from the dead, and the new creation. In other words, our mission is driven by hope that God has already accomplished his mission in the future we have not yet reached, and we are stretching out to take hold of it. Hope means living not only in the aftershock of the cross but in the "beforeshock" of the second coming. It means acting in the future present tense: we do today what we *will have done* when we give an account of ourselves before the judgment seat of Christ, straining forward to hear the words, "Well done, good and faithful servant!" (Matt. 25:21).

When Robert Coleman, author of the seminal book *The Master Plan of Evangelism*, was asked what single message he would share with today's church about making disciples, he fervently replied,

> Keep your eye on the heavenly vision. Set your perfection on things above, not on this world. Look to Jesus, who sits at the right hand of the throne of God. That's what we need to keep always in focus: it's the hope that is set before us; it's the glory that is always in the person of our Lord. . . . It's what God has called us to be. It's what he's making us to be—like him, created in his image. . . . I'm pressing on to the high calling of God in Christ Jesus. That's what he wants us to be doing in the glory of his grace.[6]

Hope like that feeds a culture of mission that erupts in more worship than a worship service ever could.

THE LAW OF POWER

Real Church Growth Is Powered by the Gospel, Not Relevance

When I was in college, I learned how to share the gospel from Campus Crusade for Christ (now called Cru). Every week for three years, I devoted time specifically to doing evangelism with my fellow Crusaders. We would walk along the line of students queued up for dinner and engage them with a spiritual interest survey. The last question on the survey was, "Would you be open to having a further conversation about Jesus?" If they said yes, we would knock on their door later that week. I kept a map of my dorm and marked every room I visited and every room whose residents had accepted Christ. To this day I get excited when I see a church that has the same sort of map of its community.

The training I received from Crusade was invaluable. It had four features critical to all genuine disciple making: modeling, practice, evaluation, and accountability. I would not be the ministry leader I am today without it.

But this great training contained a subtle trap unintended by the people who trained me. As I kept working at the practice of evangelism, I gradually slipped into believing that my skill as a communicator was an effectual part of a person coming to Christ. I did not realize it at the time, but I slowly came to believe that the more persuasive I was, the more likely it was that the other person would respond positively. If the people I talked to were going to be saved, they *needed* me to be good at evangelism.

I had stumbled into an ancient biblical tension between God's work and mine—the mystery of what it means to be God's co-worker (2 Cor. 6:1)—but I did not know it. The wheel of my ministry pulled hard to the ditch of human effort like a car with a bad tire. I learned from Crusade how to share the gospel but not how to rely on the gospel. Instead, I learned to rely on my relevance.

The Pursuit of Relevance

Thousands of churches have the mindset that I had as a college student. They believe the gospel and they share the gospel, but functionally they do not rely on the gospel to bring people into the kingdom. They rely on the relevance of their Lower Room.

For a time "relevance" was a very cool ministry word. It is not as cool now—it may have jumped the shark about the time that North Point Ministries produced its hilarious, satirical "Contemporvant" video in 2010 (fusing the terms "contemporary" and "relevant").[1] But the concept of relevance remains alive and well.

By "relevance," I mean everything churches do that they think will draw a crowd of people, hold them long enough to feed them the gospel, and make them want to swallow it. It is the secret sauce of gaining people's attention and attendance. It is hoped to reduce wariness and skepticism, to open eyes and ears, and to keep people loitering long enough to meet Jesus and be changed—provided the relevance remains relevant, that is.

Relevance is in the eye of the consumer, and the consumer's eye wanders. So church leaders are driven to exhaustion keeping up with the ever-evolving consumer's standard of relevance—or at least up with the standard of churches that try especially hard to be relevant. Some churches simply try to keep up with the standard of relevance of the people they already have, which may mean they do not change much at all. In any case, relevance is embodied in the things we do to give the people what they want—or what we think they want, or what we would want if we were in their shoes—so that they will eventually follow Jesus. This is just a partial list; you may want to highlight the ones you can relate to:

1. Amazing visual brand and savvy social media
2. Stellar communicator/preacher/teacher (whichever term you prefer)
3. Next steps class to your dream team (volunteer corps)
4. The perfect mix of demographic diversity on stage
5. Baristas serving sustainable coffee
6. Intellectual, thought-provoking services
7. Ubercool kids' ministry that your children can't wait to attend
8. VIP parking with gifts for guests
9. Heart-pumping opening worship with a face-melting band
10. Magnificent choir backed by an orchestra of virtuosos
11. Prime piece of real estate in the community
12. Topical preaching
13. Expository preaching
14. Suit and tie preacher
15. Skinny jeans preacher
16. Just enough pop culture references in sermons
17. Advanced stage lighting with lasers and fog machine
18. Visible tattoos
19. Vintage liturgy
20. Staff with advanced degrees
21. Staff with no degrees

22. Staff with "a past"

23. Youth sports leagues

24. Art displayed on every wall

Full disclosure: the consulting I've done over the years has helped churches establish and improve a number of the items on this list, and we endorse the value of many others. So what's the problem?

The problem is in a word I have already used several times in this chapter: the word "rely."

Ashamed of the Gospel

Three years after college I started seminary, where I reconnected with an intelligent mentor and high school teacher named Helen Martin. Helen loaded me up with a special gift of books that blew my Crusade-built mind and rocked my evangelistic world. Two classics that made an especially big impact were Walter Chantry's *Today's Gospel* and J. I. Packer's *Evangelism and the Sovereignty of God*.[2] Those books detonated dynamite at the foundation of my assumptions about ministry.

As I studied and pondered, I kept being led to one Bible verse in particular, Romans 1:16. It was a familiar Scripture—I had it memorized, so I thought I knew it. But now I saw that it had gone over my head; I didn't know it nearly as well as I thought I did.

Paul says in Romans 1:16 that the gospel "is the power of God that brings salvation to everyone who believes." Almost every word of this phrase was a revelation to me.

The gospel is *power*. It wasn't an inert object that I handed off to other people. It wasn't even a tool in my hand. It is a moving, pulsing, driving entity, a force unto itself.

The gospel is the power *of God*. I didn't put energy into it; God did. And if it is *his* power, it is infinitely powerful, the mightiest power on earth. It is sufficient for anything God intends it for.

The gospel is the power of God that *brings salvation*. There is one rare place where Paul says he saves people (1 Cor. 9:22), but the predominant message of the New Testament is that the gospel does it, Christ does it, God does it. There is very little evidence that I was doing it.

The gospel is the power of God that brings salvation to everyone who *believes*. Surely that was where I got involved, right? My job was to get people to believe, then the gospel could do its powerful thing. But the more I thought about it, the less that made sense. People tend to believe what they want to believe; they listen to what they want to listen to. When people don't like something, they will come up with any excuse, no matter how flimsy, not to believe it. I realized that I did not have the key to the instrument panel of a person's heart where I could flip the belief switch. Only a supernatural power—the power of God—could dispose someone to believe. And that is what Paul said the gospel is.

I had been so focused on persuading people who did not believe in the gospel for their salvation that I failed to see that I did not believe in it for their salvation either. I was so focused on bringing people to faith in the gospel that I could not see *my* lack of faith in the gospel.

I came to see that the gospel did the work to save people. It was plenty strong enough without my help. I noticed that Paul often called himself a minister, literally a servant (*diakonos*), of the gospel. I realized that my job was to serve the gospel to people the way a waiter serves a meal. My job was to bring the gospel to the table and let it do the rest.

Then I looked again at Romans 1:16, and I noticed something that cut me to the heart. Paul wrote, "I am *not ashamed* of the gospel." I thought about the queasy feeling I sometimes got when I was doing my weekly evangelism runs in college, afraid that someone would laugh at me or slam the door on me. Paul knew better than I did what it was like to be mocked and ostracized for the gospel, so I thought that was the kind of shame he meant.

I do think the shame of social rejection has something to do with it, but I also think there is more to it. Paul said that he was not ashamed of the gospel *because* it is the *power* of God that brings salvation. That must mean that Paul *would* have been ashamed of the gospel if it lacked power, *if it did not work*. And that in turn implied that if Paul relied on some other power to save people, that would have proven that he was ashamed of the gospel.

That was it. Everything about Paul's life suddenly snapped into place. That is why he fought so fiercely against requiring Gentiles to be circumcised: that requirement implied that the gospel did not work. That is why he did not come to the Corinthians "with eloquence or human wisdom" (1 Cor. 2:1): it would have implied that the gospel did not work. That is why he considered his birth status and Torah piety "garbage" (Phil. 3:8): relying on them would imply that the gospel did not work. Paul went out of his way to reject anything that might give a person a reason to think that the gospel was not all-powerful to save. To do otherwise would betray a lack of faith in the gospel's power. It would show that he was ashamed of the gospel, embarrassed by its insufficiency.

Then came the question from the Spirit that nailed me between the eyes: *Am I ashamed of the gospel?*

Think hard about this question for yourself and your own church. Look at the list above. How many items there silently suggest that you are embarrassed by the gospel?

What are you really relying on to save people?

What are you really relying on to save people? Craig Groeschel, the lead pastor of Life. Church, has popularized two slogans that get repeated in the culture of his church: "We will do anything short of sin to reach people who don't know Christ" and "To reach people no one is reaching, we'll do things no one is doing."[3] I appreciate Craig Groeschel's passion and I personally trust his heart. I have been present when he teaches this value and when he trains believers to share the gospel. More than a few churches, however, blur the fine line between do-whatever-it-takes platform maneuvers and not being ashamed of the gospel. I now believe that lots of Sunday creativity—from eye-popping props to outlandish stunts—is driven by unhealthy bravado masking shame in the gospel.

I recently attended a worship service during rodeo season in a Southwest town. The service included fifteen minutes to hold a best-Western-dressed contest for boys, girls, men, and women. Those who got the most applause in each category were given a prize. Was this worship element too cute or too far?

That same week a controversy broke regarding the speaker lineup at the Southern Baptist Convention's annual pastors' conference. One speaker is known to use edgy pop-culture references in worship. For example, the church put on a sermon series titled "Victorious Secret" utilizing a graphic that clearly mirrored the fashion lingerie brand Victoria's Secret. I discussed the controversy with a dozen church leaders at lunch one day. Half of them were inspired and half were disgusted. Did the sermon series title and graphics cross a line?

Christopher Benek makes an intense evaluation in the context of reviewing a church's financial investment in big buildings and creative programming:

> The modern church has largely forsaken the gospel to perpetuate the institution. . . . We have constructed edifices far too large and expensive to maintain. In so doing, we have forsaken the weightier teachings of Jesus focused on discipleship and helping the poor. For example, we have turned many churches into nothing more than glorified entertainment clubs that numb the self-inflicted pain of pride and greed. Instead of helping people develop a new hermeneutic of life and ultimate meaning in this technological age, we perpetuate insufficient theology that leaves people feeling helpless and without hope. We then wonder why so many churches are stagnant if not declining today in the United States.[4]

Please know that I want your church to have meaningful engagement with quality worship music. I also want your church to have an effective website and digital tools to help people find the front door. But when you stack up the entirety of what churches do to draw a crowd, there is a great gulf of embarrassment to cross to admit that they play no role in real church growth. In fact, nothing you rely on other than the gospel works to change lives. This is the scandal of Program Church: leaders come to rely more and more on Lower Room relevance for church success as they get more and more embarrassed by the gospel alone.

Drawing a Crowd

A reader might protest, "Of course the gospel alone saves people. We aren't relying on anything else to do that. We rely on those other devices to bring unbelievers in so that they will hear the gospel and believe and be saved. If we could draw a crowd just by preaching the gospel, we would, but that's not the society we live in anymore. Today you have to draw a crowd with relevance and then preach the gospel."

I reply that this response might be true if real church growth starts with a culture of worship. But it doesn't; real church growth starts with a culture of mission. And, for this reason, the one problem every church does *not* have is drawing a crowd.

You might think I'm crazy. Haven't I repeatedly talked about the decline of church attendance in North America? How can I claim that churches do not have a problem drawing a crowd?

It all comes down to what we mean by a "crowd."

> **The one problem every church does *not* have is drawing a crowd.**

In the Gospels, when Jesus is followed by a "crowd" or "crowds," it certainly means a large number of people. But that is not all the crowd was: "the crowd" could also mean the mass of people outside the inner circle—the common people as opposed to the ruling authorities. To the Judean elite, "the crowd" meant the vast bulk of Jews who were less holy and less learned than they were. For example, in John 7:49, the chief priests and Pharisees say, "This crowd that does not know the law is accursed" (ESV).

Even Jesus thought of the crowd as the outsiders who were less holy and less learned than the insiders. The revolutionary difference is that Jesus taught that anyone who believed and obeyed him, whatever their past or education or social standing, became an insider.

The important thing is that, from this angle, the crowd is not about *quantity of people* but about *quality of people*. If you are with one solitary person who is outside the kingdom of God and does not understand its mysteries—as Jesus was with the woman at the well in John 4—then you are with the crowd.

When you look at it this way, it becomes obvious that each of the believers in our churches has already drawn a crowd, a microcrowd. Each of us has crowd people among those who come and go through our presence. Granted, some believers are so entwined in a relational web of Christians that they have very few of the crowd within arm's length. But even for those believers, crowd people are usually still visible if they stand on tiptoe to see them.

The crowd is there. We do not have to go get them; we are already living among them. We do not have to entice them to come to us; they are already drawn to us, whether by sheer circumstance, natural chemistry, or divine compulsion. It does not matter whether or not the gospel draws a crowd. The gospel is not meant to draw a crowd. The gospel is meant to be given to the crowd we already have.[5]

When you structure your church's ministry, when you plan your delivery of the gospel, what audience do you picture? Do you picture the crowd in the big room, or do you picture the "crowd cloud"—the innumerable, invisible multitude of people who have personal relationships with the people in the big room? Do you see the scope of gospel impact where your worship attenders live, work, and play each day?

For example, think of a pastor who preaches to one hundred adults on a typical Sunday. Now imagine that the average person in the audience has regular contact with twenty people outside the church, whether at work, in their families, in regular businesses they frequent, in their neighborhoods, or anywhere else. The crowd cloud for that audience, then, would be two thousand people. The question is, does the pastor see their sphere of ministry impact as the one hundred or the two thousand?

Are you beginning to grasp the enormous difference? No matter how big a crowd you draw, it will always be dwarfed by the crowd cloud Jesus has given your church to reach with the gospel. The crowd cloud is bigger than the crowd before your eyes, but which is bigger in your mind?

No doubt there are church leaders who think about the crowd cloud, but many of them think about it instrumentally. That is, they think of it as a means to the gathered church as the end. They do not think of it as their audience right where it is; they think of it as a herd to be driven into the worship barn where each head can be branded, tagged, fed, and milked.

I am calling leaders to lift their vision higher. When leaders move from seeing the church as the crowd gathered in one place one day of the week to a people moving among the crowd in every place every day of the week, the unbearable burden of relevance drops away. The church is freed to return to its true power for salvation, the gospel of Christ, and to take that power everywhere it goes.

The Power of a Fully Connected Gospel

Have you ever seen a toy that lets kids put simple electrical circuits together? One version comes with a booklet that contains over a hundred schematics of different circuit designs. When you snap the connectors, transformers, switches, buttons, and other implements onto the powered board, a fan spins, a buzzer sounds, or a diode lights—or even all at the same time. But the circuit only gets power when it is connected according to the schematic. If one part remains disconnected from the circuit design, no power flows and nothing happens.

In a similar way, a major reason church leaders are tempted to seek power from so-called relevance rather than from the gospel is that their gospel is missing pieces—or, much more often, all the pieces are present but they are not all connected, so nothing lights up. They believe the gospel, but they have not put it all together in a way that lets the power flow.

> Many leaders believe the gospel, but they have not put it all together in a way that lets the power flow.

To illustrate, consider a framework of the gospel that has become familiar to many over the past decade: the four-movement biblical plotline of creation, fall, redemption, and new creation.[6] It is an excellently balanced, beautifully concise summary of the gospel, and every church leader we know agrees that the gospel contains all four movements.

The problem is that few leaders have connected all the parts of the gospel circuit. Even though everyone agrees with the basic biblical plotline in principle, each person has their own favorite part of it that they play up, which accidentally leaves the rest behind. More precisely, leaders (and churches and faith tribes) tend to pick favorite pairs from the four-part gospel sequence. Many leaders, especially among the Reformed, are fall-redemption types; self-described fundamentalists tend this way too. Many other leaders are creation–new creation types, from peace-and-justice progressives to charismatics and faith-movement preachers.

But for the gospel to be the power of God for salvation, all four movements must receive equal attention; none can be soft-pedaled or subordinated to another. When the whole gospel circuit is connected, all parts equally prominent, the release of power for the church is enormous. But when part of the sequence is missing, there is always a loss of power for salvation, mission, and discipleship.

When creation is not connected, we lose Christ as the Word—the Logos, the Reason, the Logic, the Blueprint—through whom all things were made. We lose our message that every human being has profound, sacred value—rights even—as a unique person created in God's image. We lose natural law as the basis of the laws of nations and a commonly shared understanding of right and wrong. We lose our connection to the genuine enjoyment of things of this life that we share with all people—food, drink, friends, play, romance. We lose the ingenious social structure of the family. We lose the practical knowledge represented in the book of Proverbs and in scientific inquiry that is accessible to all people. We lose art; we lose skill. And we lose the opportunity to find common ground with the genuine but fragmentary truth in other religions and philosophies as Paul did when he spoke at the Areopagus in Athens (Acts 17:16–34). We lose our kinship with all people of every race in the human race.

When the fall is not connected, we lose Christ as the Victim. We lose our capacity to explain why things don't work the way they are supposed to—why you can follow the rules and still get hurt, why you can follow your heart and still go unsatisfied. We lose our ability to name evil as evil and to point out the reality and activity of the devil. We lose sympathy and solidarity with people who are exploited and abused by people with more power, and we lose our courage to call it out. But we also lose the insight that all of us have power over someone or something, and all of us abuse it—that all of us, strongest to weakest, contribute to the evil of the world and to our own problems, and none of us can stop ourselves. We lose a clear-eyed diagnosis of the universal human addiction to our appetites, our ambitions, and the approval of others, and we lose a realistic appreciation of the nearly infinite, stubborn resistance to truth in every human heart, doomed without help from the outside. We cannot cogently express how Christ is both the innocent victim of all the world's abusive evil and the sacrificial victim without whom the debt we have racked up against justice cannot be satisfied. And we lose the urgency of imminent judgment hanging over all our heads and eternal hell yawning under our feet.

When redemption is not connected, we lose Christ as the Mediator between God and humanity, the only perfect high priest who puts us in right standing with God the Father by shedding his own blood as the perfect sacrifice. We lose the truth that no one gets anywhere on their own—that they need a helper, a do-over, a huge favor they can't repay, a second chance they can't screw up, a way in with the person in charge, a test with their name at the top that someone else filled in with all the right answers—in other words, grace. We lose the way for people to get out from under the oppressive weight of what they have done and who they are, and the truth that no one gets out without being carried out. We lose the truth that no one gets to the happy ending without losing all their pride and making no boast except in the sufficiency of Christ. And we lose the glorious reality that all suffering is bearable when you know that the Father looks on you the way he looks on his Son.

When new creation is not connected, we lose Christ as Savior, the victorious King who replaces this world with a restoration better than the original. We lose hope. We lose the promise that we have more than a good name with God; we have a certainty of endless bliss. We lose the confidence that we will one day tangibly become the people God says we are. And perhaps most importantly, we lose the faith that we can taste that experience *right now*—that genuine transformation, real deliverance, and authentic healing of body and mind happens now by the power of the Holy Spirit. We lose the claim that associating with Christ actually, objectively improves your life, not just what you happen to think about your life. We lose the proposal that whole communities and even nations can experience social and physical renewal as a foretaste of the kingdom of God. We lose the affirmation that people's yearning for a happy ending is not a childhood fantasy but is more real than anything they have ever known in this life.

Do you glimpse the power of a fully connected gospel? A gospel with all four pieces connected, all movements expressed and believed in equal balance, powers mission. It establishes common ground, appreciation, and enjoyment between believers and unbelievers (creation); it provides a sympathetic, realistic, and complete diagnosis of the human condition (fall); it extends radical grace and mercy to everyone who wants a new start (redemption); and it promises a better future and a better present than anyone else has come up with (new creation). How is that not relevant?

Think of the power of the fully connected gospel for disciples. It gives practical counsel compatible with all the knowledge people could ever discover (creation); it trains disciples to ruthlessly fight their own sin, not to lean on their own understanding, and to be realistic about resistance from a hostile world (fall); it enables them to live in freedom, with patience and gratitude, in the confidence of who they are in Christ (redemption); and it is the conduit of power from the throne of God to change their world and fill them with joyful hope (new creation). How is that not relevant?

As Bill Hull and Ben Sobels say, "The gospel you preach determines the disciples you make."[7] A gospel with all movements equally prominent, all parts fully connected, releases power in and through believers to be disciples who make disciples. In other words, a complete gospel, completely proclaimed, empowers real church growth.

The Gospel: A New Mind for Ministry

Paul observed to the Corinthians that the Jews and Greeks of his day each had their idea of relevance. "Jews demand signs and

Greeks look for wisdom." But Paul did not rely on relevance to attract their attention and win them over. Rather, "we preach Christ crucified: a stumbling block to Jews and foolishness to Gentiles." Nevertheless, "to those whom God has called, both Jews and Greeks," Christ is not a barrier but a booster: "the power of God and the wisdom of God" (1 Cor. 1:22–24).

The leader who breaks through to reliance on the gospel for salvation gains a new mind, "the mind of Christ" (2:16). Then ministry changes in all sorts of ways.

When I came to believe that the gospel really is the power of God for salvation, it turned up my confidence and motivation as an evangelist. I remember thinking, "Wow, I get to go out and discover who God is wooing to himself. My evangelism isn't about my skill; it's about seeing whose hearts the Holy Spirit is already working in." Evangelism is almost like a child's game where a ball is hidden under a shell. Because of the gospel, I knew there was a ball under a shell somewhere, so I just kept sharing the gospel until I found the ball.

Reliance on the gospel in the Upper Room changes how we do everything in the Lower Room. We still gather people to worship, but we remember that God is the one we are worshiping, so we plan it to delight him, not the crowd. We still show hospitality in all sorts of ways to those who attend, but we do it because we love them, not because we want to assimilate them. In fact, we show hospitality at worship more easily when we have been showing hospitality to our microcrowds all week long; hospitality becomes who we are, so we are always on the lookout for the ball under the shell wherever we are.

In other words, when we stop being ashamed of the gospel, we still do much of the ministry stuff we did before with a standard of excellence, but we do it with a different spirit and for a different reason. We do it to love God and love our neighbor, not just to grow our attendance. At the same time, we stop the relentless pursuit of doing anything that only tries to draw in or pamper the crowd we already move among every day. We abandon our reliance on relevance.

The church has nothing to offer the world in the way of relevance; the world can always find a more pleasing alternative elsewhere. The one thing the church has to offer is the one thing that is relevant to every person in every age: the eternal gospel of Jesus Christ, the power of God for salvation to everyone who believes. Church leaders need to believe it ourselves, because Future Church will not be known for the glamour of its show but for the splendor of its faith.

THE LAW OF LOVE

Real Church Growth Is Validated by Unity, Not Numbers

I n chapter 3 I presented five reasons that church leaders unintentionally stay stuck in a functional mission other than Jesus's mission. I said that our functional mission is displayed in what we measure. Leaders are prone to measure the inputs of worship attendance and giving and sometimes the throughputs of small group participation and volunteers. In other words, we usually count the bodies that pass into and through the ministry machine.

In that earlier chapter I said that we measure input results because they are easy to measure. But that leaves a deeper question unanswered: *Why do we measure anything at all?*

Think about this for a second. People do not count themselves. Even if attendance is the low-hanging fruit of measurement, you still have to pick it off the tree. So why do you take the trouble to do it?

You may do it because other ministry leaders have modeled it to you; it's just what you do. You may have various practical justifications for it. But I believe that there is another motive lurking in all of us who count attenders: we want to validate our efforts.

This motive is the most natural thing in the world, and it is not a bad one either. "That every man who eats and drinks sees good in all his labor—it is the gift of God" (Eccles. 3:13 NASB). It is a blessing to see that your work has produced good results; in fact, no one can go on working forever unless they get that validation.

For instance, there are many people, including many pastors, who love to mow the lawn. (Apologies to those who live in places where there are no lawns.) What is a burdensome chore to others is sheer delight to them. When they start the job, the lawn looks bad. When they finish, the lawn looks good. They can see the results plain as day; they made a difference for the better, and they know it.

What a refreshing relief the lawn is from a week spent in ministry! Ministry is notorious for withholding clear results from those who practice it. Spiritual growth takes a long time. It is not easily seen or measured (though, as I pointed out, measuring is not impossible). It often looks like three steps forward and two (or more) steps back. It can be as changeable, intangible, and cloudy as fog.

Numbers, on the other hand, are black and white, clear, objective. They are easily depicted on a graph. And rising numbers imply everything from increasing momentum to rising popularity. We naturally want to validate our efforts and to recognize when a course correction is needed, and numbers are begging to do the job for us. Because of the long tradition of practicality in the evangelical church, we usually take them up on it. But our judgment is clouded by our pragmatic obsession with what works to bring people in, so we avoid asking whether our numbers really prove that we are making disciples.

Take this case in point: a 2019 podcast episode in which the host interviewed senior staff of a leading megachurch. To its credit, this church throughout its history has prioritized the outsider over the insider; evangelism is highly important to church leaders, and baptisms are counted as zealously as attendance. For years those numbers validated that the church was on the right track. As one leader put it, it used to be "easy to look at the metrics and say, 'Yeah, this is working.'"

So it was unprecedented and disturbing when the church's numbers started to level off. The leaders did some serious soul-searching and made changes to the worship service: less Top 40 music, more songs with lyrics a newcomer might not entirely understand, more prayer, more public testimonies of God's supernatural work in people's lives.

But the slight shift toward a more conventionally Christian worship service is not the interesting thing; the reason for the shift is. As the host put it, "The way we did it isn't the way we're doing it because it's not connecting the way it was." Leaders saw their friends leaving attractional churches for options that were more "ancient" and "gritty," and they did not want to "look back ten years from now and say, 'We missed the cultural change and the trends that were happening.'" In other words, they changed worship in large part because the market demanded it.

Rising numbers appeared to validate the changes they made. The host remarked, "The last time I connected with you guys you had just had a record Sunday in attendance. People are being drawn here and finding God."[1]

I sincerely hope and believe that is true, and I thank God for it. (And I believe that the podcast participants are 100 percent genuine in their desire to see lost people saved.) But note what is *not* said. The proof that the worship adjustments were the right move is not that the presence of God can be felt in the room as never before or that worshipers are living holier lives or that persecution from ungodly people is increasing or—perhaps most importantly—that they have more disciple makers than they used to. It is that attendance is climbing again.

Of course we want to see the number of Jesus's disciples increase the way it did in the book of Acts. But the scandal of our time is that we have made attendance, the numerical by-product of disciple making, into the proof of disciple making even though we may not be making disciples at all.

For the sake of real church growth, we need to stop measuring our efforts against a target number of 100 or 400 or 1,000 or 4,000 or 10,000 or 40,000. Instead, we should measure our churches against a different number—the number 1.

The Math of Real Church Growth

When Lower Room numbers are validating our efforts, we operate with a math equation lurking below the surface of our thoughts. It looks something like this:

$$1 + 1 + 1 + \cdots = n$$

What is n? Who knows? All we know is that we have to keep adding more and more until we reach the goal we will never reach. Simply put, our ministry target is just one more: $[+1]$.

Now compare the standard church growth equation to God's Upper Room math:

$$1 + 1 + 1 = 1$$

This is the mysterious math of the Trinity: one fully divine person plus another plus another equals one God.

I don't present this equation as a theological trump card. Instead, I share it because the math of the Trinity is the supreme church growth equation. Jesus himself taught us that if we master—rather, if we are mastered by—the math of God's nature, we will experience church growth beyond our wildest dreams.

Jesus's church growth math class is a prayer—the longest of his prayers that we have in writing, John 17.

The first truth Jesus speaks of in John 17 is that he and his Father have been *one* forever in heaven, but now we get to see this reality on earth. Their *oneness* is about sharing their glory back and forth—the Father glorifies the Son by giving him authority, and the Son glorifies the Father by giving him obedience (vv. 1–5).

Second, Jesus's disciples are different from the rest of the world, because they believe that Jesus and his Father are *one*, as Jesus told them. Disciples belong to the Father now in a special way that the world does not grasp (vv. 6–10).

Third, the Father and the Son took the *oneness*, the joy, and the truth that circulates in their give-and-take of glory and put it in Jesus's disciples. Now the disciples are *one* and are full of joy and truth themselves. They have to be—these are their assets and their armor as they go on a mission into a hostile and unbelieving world (vv. 11–19).

Last comes the church growth payoff. The Father and the Son are drawing all who believe the disciples' message into their own *oneness*. They are making us as *one* as they are as they make us *one* with themselves. As we display *oneness*—unity—throngs of people are drawn out of the world into us and into God (vv. 20–26; see figure 3).[2]

Figure 3 - John 17:20-26

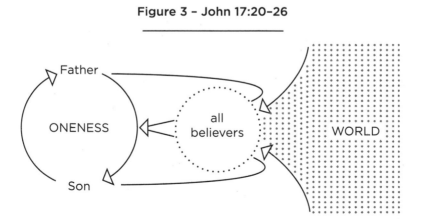

Don't miss this: when it comes to growth, *the church's number one asset is the number 1*—our unity. Jesus requested "that all of them may be one, Father, just as you are in me and I am in you . . . so that the world may believe that you have sent me" (John 17:20–21). People believe in Jesus when we are one. This is what Jesus requires to complete the mission he started in the world.

The target of real church growth, then, is not [+1]. It is [=1]. When we reach [=1], it is not only proof that we have really grown; it is our growth engine until Jesus returns.

What Is Unity?

Unfortunately, it is easier to count heads than to weigh love. So if real church growth is validated by unity, how do we spot it?

A fuller definition of unity helps us recognize it when we see it. Think of unity as the high bridge between pairs of opposites, the both-and beyond false either-ors.

Unity Is the Bridge between Orthodoxy and Orthopraxy

Unity is more than orthodoxy, but it certainly is not less. The word "orthodoxy" comes from Greek words for "upright thinking." It is likely that none of us thinks perfectly right, but if we are all on a quest toward that goal and we keep from falling into a ditch of falsehood on either side of the road, we walk as one.

Early in the missional orientation, however, at the same time the gospel-centered movement was rising, certain voices under the label "emergent" reacted against orthodoxy and challenged its value. They said that what was much more important was *orthopraxy*, meaning "upright action"—deeds, not creeds. The idea was that if we are all showing the love for people that Jesus commanded, then we will all be one.

And so the quarrel began, like the left hand and the right hand arguing about which is more important for clapping.

I say that true unity is neither orthodoxy nor orthopraxy—or, if you like, it is the union of both. What reconciles orthodoxy and orthopraxy is *orthostasis*.

Orthostasis is not a made-up word. It is a medical term that comes from the Greek for "upright standing." Orthostasis is the doctors' word for standing up straight. Orthostasis is ideal when a person's posture is good and all the parts of their body are properly aligned.

The church gets its orthodoxy right and its orthopraxy right only when its orthostasis is right—only when the parts of the body of Christ relate to one another the right way.

If you are familiar with Paul's letter to the Ephesians, you have probably noticed a pattern in that book. The first half (chapters 1–3) appears to be about orthodoxy, believing the right thing. The second half (chapters 4–6) appears to be about orthopraxy, doing the right thing. But if you look again, you see that Ephesians is actually a *three*-part book. Set between the right-thinking beginning and the right-doing end is the right-standing middle.

Beginning in Ephesians 2:11 Paul describes how Jews and Gentiles, who were hostile toward each other, have now been reconciled in one body of Christ through the cross, which makes all of them members of God's household (family). In chapter 3 Paul describes his mission to preach this truth to Jews and Gentiles to make them one, and he prays that *every* family on mission in *all* God's holy people would know Christ's love that defies comprehension. In chapter 4 he urges believers to "be completely humble and gentle; be patient, bearing with one another in love," to "make every effort to keep the unity of the Spirit through the bond of peace" (vv. 2–3). He describes how the oneness of the church includes a variety of giftings that *together* "equip his people for works of service" (orthopraxy) "so that the body of Christ may be built up until we all reach unity in the faith" (orthodoxy; vv. 12–13).

The phrase that captures it all is "speaking the truth in love." When our right thinking (truth) cooperates perfectly with our right acting (love), *"we will grow* to become in every respect the mature body of him who is the head, that is, Christ" (v. 15, emphasis added). A body standing upright—orthostasis. That is what we call *real church growth*.

So as you try to validate your efforts in ministry, ask these questions about your church's unity:

- Do we excel at both right thinking *and* right acting?
- Do we humbly, gently, patiently, lovingly, peaceably make every effort to keep the unity of the Spirit?

Unity Is the Alternative to Superficiality and Uniformity

Contrary to the stereotype of infamous fights over the color of the carpet, unity is important to many churches. However, many churches settle for merely getting along, which is less than the unity Jesus prayed for and the Holy Spirit makes possible. They limp along together without talking about their differences that simmer below the surface because every family is getting paid off by place, programs, a personality, or (most of all) the social comfort of other people. But superficiality is not unity in Christ. You don't deserve much credit for unity if you never say anything a person could disagree with.

On the other hand, some churches talk about all sorts of issues, but they require agreement on all of them. The classic example is when churches major on the minors—when they make doctrinal, ethical, or political positions of secondary importance into hills to die on. (The eternal challenge, of course, is figuring out which issues are majors and which ones are minors.)

But this tendency also shows itself in some churches that seem broad and accepting on the surface. Some churches do not grind an axe over doctrine, but they do quietly compel conformity to their values or culture or style. To get somewhere in the church, or even to really belong, it helps to talk a certain way, pray a certain way, educate your kids a certain way, read a certain sort of book, drive a certain sort of car, work a certain sort of job, wear a certain sort of clothes or hairstyle, watch a certain sort of TV show.

The same phenomenon can appear when churches hire staff. It is not uncommon to find one church where every staff member is Winston Churchill and another where everyone is Fred Rogers. A certain personality image becomes the touchstone for what a "real" pastor is. Or the common denominator may be jargon— everyone has read the same books and gone to the same conferences, has the same heroes and formative influences, and talks the same way. Uniformity may descend from a lead pastor who wants staff members who do exactly what they would do. Most pastors mistake uniformity for team chemistry. Chemistry requires different perspectives; uniformity never allows them. Chemistry combines the strengths of many; uniformity clones the strengths of one.

Most pastors mistake uniformity for team chemistry.

The danger is that a leadership team can suffocate by groupthink. When a leadership team's stance is dangerously narrow, a new challenge makes it wobble. Worse, when leaders are chosen based primarily on the lead pastor's image instead of Christ's, the people of the church see no unity that they cannot see anywhere else in the world.

Unity in Christ is not uniformity. As the first-century church took root in the diverse cities of the Roman Empire, one of its great advantages was that it was too small to self-segregate on ethnicity, class, education, or personal style. When outsiders looked at the church, they saw a group composed of a bewildering diversity of people who laid down their lives for each other because of this strange Jew called Christus. They had never seen anything like it; there was no parallel. Some were awed by it, some were drawn to it, some were repulsed by it, but no one could ignore it.

Once again, as you try to validate your efforts in ministry, ask these questions about your church:

- Do we regularly open up with each other even on issues that make us uncomfortable because we may disagree?
- Is the range of personal styles of our people broad enough to reflect the breadth of the kingdom of God in our locale?
- Are the perspectives of our leaders as diverse (and complementary) as the perspectives of the various authors of Scripture?
- Do we appreciate alternative perspectives by investing in dialogue that produces a deeper unity amidst diversity?

Read about the third "both-and" of unity—the paradox of acceptance and accountability—at futurechurchbook.com/bonus.

The Attraction of Unity

You may be beginning to recognize the dilemma faced by the growing church. For growth to be validated by orthostasis—biblical unity and love—people have to know each other deeply. But the larger the church gets, the harder it is to know others and be known by them. This is another reason why real church growth is not validated by numbers: growth can be the counterfeit of grace because quantity is the enemy of intimacy.

Jesus's John 17 prayer for unity forces us to revise our understanding of what church growth looks like. The mission is still to seek and save the lost, to bring in a harvest, to bear witness to the ends of the earth. But the church truly grows as fast as it multiplies the *oikos* (household) of God, not as fast as it builds a cool building. The world does not see real church growth in a new [+1] facility, even though sometimes it is genuinely worthwhile to build one. The world sees real church growth in a new [=1] fellowship gathered in their neighbor's backyard, where the good and the bad get a foretaste of the feast of the kingdom of God.

As long as we are living in the Lower Room of Program Church, we have no chance to arrive at [=1], because we are driven by our own individual needs and preferences. But if we are united in the Upper Room mission to make disciples of all the nations, we have a chance of reaching [=1]. The irony is that if we live in the Upper Room, we are validated by how unified we are in reaching people, not by how many people we reach. But according to Jesus's prayer, that is precisely how we reach the most.

Our mission determines our measures. Program Church counts what's inside; Future Church counts what's outside. If my church's culture is centered in gathering people to worship services, the number of people at my church tells the tale of success—especially as it's measured against the number of people at your church. But if my church's culture is centered on mission to the world, it opens up all kinds of possibilities for unity. I start measuring things beyond myself, such as the percentage of unbelievers in our city or the number of people in poverty. Then, in light of the dire need of the lost and the immensity of the task, most differences between believers, congregations, and faith tribes seem insignificant. It becomes apparent that all of us have to pull together as one to reach our entire community.

Make no mistake. True unity is not a walk in the park. True love is so messy that it does not immediately convert to attractional growth. But it is so beautiful that it attracts more than any show or marketing ever could.

I confess that as I look back over my career and calling to the church, I have struggled more to keep this law than to keep any other. I feel convicted about times I've prized numbers over love. The challenge I face—that we all face—is expressed in this question: If you were given the choice between more people or more unity in your church next Sunday, which would you take?

THE LAW OF CONTEXT

Real Church Growth Is Local, Not Imported

There's a scene in the 1995 film *Smoke* where Brooklyn cigar shop owner Auggie (played by Harvey Keitel) reveals to a customer what he calls his "life's work." Every morning at eight o'clock, without fail, in all kinds of weather, Auggie takes one picture of his corner storefront from the opposite corner of the intersection. He keeps the developed photos neatly in a series of photo albums, carefully marked with the date, going back almost two decades.

His customer Paul (William Hurt) can't understand why he does it. "They're all the same," he says as he pages through, mystified. Auggie corrects him. "You'll never get it if you don't slow down, my friend. . . . They're all the same, but each one is different from every other one." As Paul slows down to look at the pictures more carefully, he begins to see subtle but rich diversity in the photos. The light is different. The weather is different. Some people in frame only appear once in the album while others appear again and again. Auggie's one, hyperlocal vantage point reveals a whole world that Paul could not see if he did not slow down to look.

Auggie's overwhelming photographic archive depicted the slow, steady flow of change in a community over twenty years. How has your community changed over the last twenty years? Answers vary from community to community, of course, and there are various ways to respond. Yet perhaps you have seen a trend that I have observed: the revival of all things local.

For example, over the last two years, the 1980s shopping mall in my suburb of Houston has been undergoing a local transformation. One of its new restaurants, Whiskey Cake, is a farm-to-table enterprise that grows its herbs in the mall parking lot. Yes, fast food is still everywhere, but it's old. The local chef is new. Consistency everywhere is being displaced by the flavor of somewhere.

What does local cuisine and urban development have to do with Future Church? As it turns out, everything.

Can a Big Box Be Too Big?

In the new permission era, church growth evolved the way community growth evolved. As suburbs multiplied, suburban people became accustomed to driving considerable distances at high speeds to a big-box store to shop under one roof for everything they wanted. New big-box churches catered to the same impulse.

Read more about how different ministry models reflect the last seventy years of urban planning at futurechurchbook.com/bonus.

Many new big-box churches bore the name "community church," yet they drew people from a metro region, not from a local community in any conventional sense. New permission leaders knew, however, that unless people felt more community at their church than at a Walmart, they would not keep coming back to that church. So leaders invested heavily in developing small groups that would allow their churches to get unimaginably large but still give people a dash of the community they craved. Even so, most of the small groups themselves went against the grain of localness; the church that drew from a vast territory birthed small groups that also drew from a wide area.

Only a few churches then and now were big-box churches, of course, but their influence was huge. Certain churches that positioned themselves as the leading edge produced conferences and books to display their ministry model, and other churches tried to copy it. Directly or indirectly, the innovations of big-box church informed the models of everyone and became the pacesetting model for many.

Despite its pervasive influence, the big-box church arouses strongly mixed feelings. I have witnessed this firsthand when I have been privileged to serve as a consultant to many of America's largest churches. I served a church in the Southeast with a seven-thousand-seat auditorium, fourteen acres of carpet, and its own exit off the highway. I served a church with a $120 million building in the downtown of a Texas city. I served a church with an ancient-modern feel in the suburban Midwest with a stained-glass window larger than a basketball court and a construction cost of $80 million.

There is no doubt that millions of people love these churches and others like them, or else they would not be so big. But every time I get an Uber ride to the last of these churches, the driver makes a negative comment about its size. One time a driver thought our route was taking us away from the church, and he said to me, "I'm glad you're not going to *that* monstrosity." A minute later he was dropping me off at the front door. I said, "What would you think if I told you I was the architect?"

It is natural for people to make judgments about a church's size, but so much that divides the church is not a matter of simple right and wrong. It is about right things done for the wrong reasons or wrong things done for the right reasons.

One right reason is to reach more people for Christ, which was the burning need and holy ambition that drove the innovators of the new permission era. These leaders inherited dechurched populations living in continually expanding, car-centered suburbs, and they tailored their churches to meet that need. Having a big church was a natural result of succeeding, and it proved to be a useful asset to win still more.

Nevertheless, in this chapter I wish to consider whether it is possible to build a church that is too big—or perhaps more accurately, too nonlocal. I expect many readers to have strong, gut-level answers to that question—some yes, others no. Either way, I want you to explore with me what problems might arise when we lose local, something both big and small churches can do.

Taken Out of Context

Around the time the missional reorientation began, I carried a zeal for clarifying the unique vision lying dormant in every church that was just waiting to be put into words. One of the pillars of Vision Framing is not only the conviction that every *church* is unique but also that every church's *community context* is unique. We call it the *local predicament*.

We are passionate about the local predicament, because when the church forgets the Law of Context—that *real church growth is local, not imported*—the mission of Jesus pays the price. To the extent that the church is taken out of context:

- *The usefulness of programs is potentially mismatched.* When leaders are not emotionally connected to local problems, they can indiscriminately run solutions designed *by* someone else, somewhere else, *for* someone else—like David wearing Saul's armor (1 Sam. 17:38–39).
- *The uniqueness of setting is tragically squandered.* When it comes to both substance and style of ministry, local trumps generic. Every location has a unique story, unique features,

unique strengths, and unique possibilities. You might enjoy touring a perfect model home that is perfectly neutral, but you wouldn't want to live in it. A lived-in house or neighborhood has welcoming appeal that a generic space, no matter how well-appointed, can never match.

- *The progress of evangelism is practically distracted.* Believers have a harder time building relationships, serving, and having spiritual conversations with unbelievers when the church separates them from their neighborhoods to do church activities elsewhere.
- *The witness of unity is essentially diminished.*

The last point is a big one, because it ties directly to the Law of Love from the previous chapter. The church's number one church growth asset is [=1]; believers' unity is God's principal tool to draw lost people to himself. But the lost will only be drawn by it if they can see it, and they cannot see it when it is hidden in widely separated buildings thirty minutes away.

In Romans, Paul teaches that creation is, so to speak, God's billboard to all people advertising that he exists (Rom. 1:20; see also Ps. 19:1–4). Likewise, in John, Jesus teaches that the unity of believers is God's billboard advertising that the Father sent the Son (John 17:20–21). But when churches detach their members from the context around them, church leaders effectively saw off and take down God's unity billboard where people live, work, and play to put up their own billboard out by the highway.

In 2000, I attended a conference at Willow Creek Community Church, which at that time was running about eighteen thousand attenders a weekend. I went to a breakout session on community with Dr. Gilbert Bilezikian, a scholar, a key architect of Willow from its early days, and the author of *Community 101: Reclaiming the Local Church as a Community of Oneness.*[1] I approached him after the session and asked him a bold question: "How big was too big for Willow?"

He looked me straight in the eye and answered with authority, as if he had been waiting to be asked. "Nine thousand," he said.

I never found out what happened at the nine thousand mark to shape Bilezikian's opinion. Yet he was not the last to grapple with the problem. In 2005 Willow Creek hired Randy Frazee, lead pastor of Pantego Bible Church in Fort Worth, Texas. A major part of his mandate was to retool Willow along the lines of his book *The Connecting Church*, which set forth the neighborhood-based small groups strategy that Frazee pioneered at Pantego. But three years later, Frazee left Willow Creek with the initiative aborted.[2] Despite the initial wishes of Willow's leadership, the church's attractional operating system could not run Frazee's local software.

Going Small for Big Impact

In 1997 Lyle Schaller wrote, "One basic societal trend in North America is that institutions, like people, are larger than their counterparts of 1900 or 1945," a generalization that Schaller applied to everything from banks to bathrooms to basketball players. He observed the trend in churches as well: "The average (mean) size of a congregation is three times what it was in 1900."[3]

Schaller's observation is indisputable as it pertains to institutions. Everything *has* become bigger. But I believe that at least in some respects, we have reached and probably passed the highwater mark. Over the next twenty years, while some things will continue growing bigger, many things will intentionally become smaller, including churches. In many cases, following Jesus's example, they will become smaller to become bigger.

Dispatches from the Frontier of the Small

When you look at a community from an elevated angle like this— from the top of a ski slope or from an airplane preparing to land—it almost feels like a God's-eye view of the world. It makes me wonder what God sees when he looks at his church in a city. Does he see the separate buildings where people gather? Or does he see all the individuals he has redeemed as they go about their daily lives in factories, offices, schools, and neighborhoods? In other words, does he see the church dispersed *everywhere*—or perhaps better put, in a multitude of *somewheres*?

After three years at Willow Creek, Randy Frazee left to become senior pastor of Oak Hills Church in San Antonio as longtime pastor Max Lucado transitioned to become its teaching pastor. (I was working with Oak Hills through the Vision Framing process at the time.) Frazee was once again hired to implement a neighborhood-based small groups and outreach strategy.

Frazee's radical insight is that suburban churches miss the greatest opportunity in the kingdom by drawing attenders out of a wide expanse of neighborhoods (which he defines as no larger than about two hundred households apiece).[4] An unsaved family living between two Christian families does not see the body of Christ, because their next-door neighbors abandon the neighborhood one or more times a week for programs at different churches, each a half hour away.

Frazee issued a revolutionary instruction to members of his church: if they could only do one church activity in a week, that activity should be gathering in their neighborhood with all other believing neighbors, regardless of what church they attend on Sunday. He practiced what he preached, making major changes in his own family's lifestyle in order to facilitate greatly increased contact between themselves and their neighbors.

Frazee is now serving Westside Family Church in the greater Kansas City area, but his legacy at Oak Hills lives on. Take, for example, this excerpt from the church's statement of values:

> Imagine seeing *unity* throughout the Body of Christ and watching it extend into your *family* and *community*. Imagine *grace, truth, and*

faith planting itself in your core and broadening its roots to your relationships and interactions with every person in your life. As these bleed into your life, your *family* as the core teaching and discipling center will grow and be an example to all the families in your *neighborhood*. While people in your neighborhood see this they will want to be a part of Christ's community.[5]

In addition, after pursuing a multisite strategy linked to its neighborhood focus, Oak Hills is now endeavoring to transition from one church on many campuses to a family of independent churches by the fall of 2021, with more churches to be planted thereafter.[6] In this respect, Oak Hills typifies a trend visible also in the Redeemer Family of Churches in New York City, the Grace Family of Churches in Greater Atlanta, the Calvary Family of Churches in metropolitan Denver, and others. Multisite is on its way out; multichurch is in. The big church is deliberately getting smaller to make a bigger impact for the kingdom.

East End Fellowship in Richmond, Virginia, displays another path to the same context-intensive result. (Doug Paul is a good friend and the pastor of vision and mobilization there.) A number of families belonging to different churches lived in a neighborhood with one of the highest concentrations of poverty in the United States. They were convinced that if the kingdom of God were to be manifested there, it would look like a transformed neighborhood composed of people who were diverse in every conceivable way. These believers began meeting over a meal and the Bible once a month and later once a week. Their meetings multiplied in more homes as more neighbors took part, and they began to get all the groups together for worship once a month.

Eventually John Perkins, cofounder of the Christian Community Development Association, visited these disciples and challenged them to convert their meetings into a named church as a public witness as the body of Christ in the community. They did so and shifted their primary church affiliations from their disparate, mostly racially homogeneous churches to East End Fellowship. The church concentrates its ministry in a two-square-mile area primarily through about a dozen missional communities (House Churches).[7]

Churches like East End Fellowship and Oak Hills Church have tapped into a dynamic that was visible in Jesus's ministry: a back-and-forth cycle of Jesus going to people and people flocking to him. As summarized in Matthew 4:23, "Jesus went throughout Galilee, teaching in their synagogues, proclaiming the good news of the kingdom, and healing every disease and sickness among the people." In other words, Jesus was reaching people in their contexts. Then, as a result, "News about him spread all over Syria, and people brought to him all who were ill with various diseases . . . and he healed them. Large crowds from Galilee, the Decapolis, Jerusalem, Judea and the region across the Jordan followed him" (vv. 24–25). In other words, people from a wide area were drawn to him.

The more contextual Jesus became, the more attractional he became. The key was that he continually resisted the distraction of attraction. He was quick to leave the crowd pressing around him to go to the town farther away, and he was willing to launch all of his assistants into households on the missional frontier even if it left him alone to deal with hundreds and thousands of people by himself.

Jesus's method of mission was perfectly in keeping with what God had been doing for two thousand years and is still doing today. From Abraham on, God's mission strategy has always been to start with someone somewhere in order to reach everyone everywhere.[8]

> The more contextual Jesus became, the more attractional he became.

The Global North and West have forgotten this lesson, but it has since been learned by believers in the Global South and East. In Randy Frazee's words,

I believe our dependency on buildings and centralized structures is one of the primary reasons the individual American church has found it difficult to rise above a 25,000-member ceiling while Christian churches around the world are able to reach and exceed this number, numbering as high as 250,000 members. But this is only possible with a decentralized structure that is not dependent on physical structure.[9]

Putting *Local* Back in the Local Church

In their book *Slow Church*, Christopher Smith and John Pattison describe a phrase from French cuisine: *"le goût de terroir*, which can be translated 'the taste of the place.'"* They cite Carlo Petrini's definition of *terroir* as

"the combination of natural factors (soil, water, slope, height above sea level, vegetation, microclimate) and human ones (tradition and practice and cultivation) that gives a unique character to each small agricultural locality and the food grown, raised, made, and cooked there." Thus, a Pinot noir from Oregon's Willamette Valley takes on the taste and texture of the grape, the soil, the barrel and the late frost.

Smith and Pattison recognize a parallel between the *terroir* of food and the *terroir* of the church as God intended it. The local church, they write, "is rooted in the natural, human and spiritual cultures of a particular place. It is a distinctively local expression of the global body of Christ. 'The Word became flesh and blood, and moved into the neighborhood' (John 1:14 The Message)."[10]

The kind of church that Smith and Pattison advocate for is gritty, not glossy. It is next-door, not Six Flags over Jesus. So how do leaders get invested in their local context?

When believers think about who does mission, we tend to focus on extremes of size. On the one hand, we picture large and complex church and parachurch organizations doing mission; on the other hand, we assign the task of mission to the individual disciple of Jesus. Some pick a midway missional alternative—a small congregation or site. But in the early church as described in the New Testament, none of these were the most common units of mission, though they all have their place. Rather, the basic missional structure was the family. It is more than just one method among several valid options. Rather, the family is built into the mission of God, which is to create and redeem people into the family of God.

In New Testament times, an urban Greco-Roman family centered on its *oikos*, a Greek word that could mean "house" (a physical structure that also housed the family business), "home" (an identity structure), or "household" (a social and economic structure). To a Roman *paterfamilias* ("head of household"), his *oikos* included his wife, children, extended family, slaves, hired workers, weaker and poorer people he supported and protected, and regular vendors, customers, and business associates. In short, it was anyone he would not be surprised to see entering the gate into his *atrium* ("courtyard"). In other words, his *oikos* was the social extension of his family, his sphere of relational influence, and his web of connection. His house was the physical center of the social network.[11]

Few people headed an *oikos*, but almost everyone belonged to one. The gospel gained ground by gaining a foothold in an *oikos*, taking it over, and then spreading from one to the next. The New Testament is full of easily missed examples of this, from Paul's invitation to Philippi's jailer and his *oikos* to be saved (Acts 16:31) to the church that met in Priscilla and Aquila's *oikos* (Rom. 16:3–5) to Paul's delight that the gospel was even making inroads in the *oikos* of Caesar, which essentially served as the bureaucracy of the Roman Empire (Phil. 1:22–23; 4:22).

Threats to the stability of the nuclear family get much attention today, but the more widespread crisis is the breakdown of the *oikos*. Average household size in the United States has steadily declined over the past six decades from 3.33 persons in 1960 to

2.53 in 2018.[12] More people than ever before live alone. Worse, fewer people than ever before have regular, meaningful entry into other people's homes. Loneliness and its accompanying mental illnesses are at record highs. Never before has there been a more pressing need for believers to obey the Bible's command to practice hospitality to those around them (Rom. 12:13; 1 Pet. 4:9).[13]

The missional *oikos* isn't just a creature of the first century and the twenty-first century. Amazingly, it flourished during the new permission era as well. Think about it: the origin story of almost every megachurch born in that period involves a group of people meeting in someone's living room. For example, Clear Creek Community Church, which now has over five thousand in attendance, started with nine families who met in 1993 with Bruce and Susan Wesley in a neighborhood called South Shore.

How do we make more of these living rooms on mission? The basic method is to turn your home into a regular relational hub for believers and unbelievers alike, whether you live there with a family, with a spouse, with a roommate, or by yourself. Disciples make their homes a consistent node of connection for a variety of people that is fertile ground for deeper one-on-one relationships. Imagine how many people will step into your home who would never set foot in your church. What if the best opportunity for the mission of Jesus is that when they do step into your home, they have actually stepped into the church without realizing it? A missional *oikos* makes it much easier for the gospel to spread from person to person because it makes Christianity socially plausible to unbelievers; they can see themselves becoming Christians because they already belong with them in familiar space.

Temperance

The ancient Greeks named four virtues—like the four points of the compass—that medieval Christians adopted as some of the essentials for becoming the follower of Christ God saved us to be. One of those cardinal virtues is temperance.

Temperance basically means self-control. It means disciplining your desires and keeping them in healthy limits. It means not letting the stuff you consume, consume you. It means enjoying life without making life all about your enjoyment.

The Law of Context invites disciples to grow in temperance because it makes church something more than a dispensary of religious goods and services. Real church growth invites disciples to be producers, not just consumers. Staying local means that believers sacrifice a night of driving to church to fill up on programs—or of staying home to be glued to screens—and instead devote it to their neighbors. The great news is that after a little while, keeping me-first desires in check makes for a much more satisfying life lived on God's mission.

The Law of Context requires temperance in church leaders too. When real church growth happens—that is, when mission, power, and love work to reach people and make disciples—there is an immediate temptation to program the church and build a bigger box to accommodate more people. But the moment you step out of context, you step onto the gerbil wheel of worship, relevance, and numbers—the big Sunday show. Context, then, is the Upper Room governor that safeguards mission, power, and love in the Lower Room by keeping them local, distributed, and among the people. How to develop those people as salt and light in their local context is the subject of the next chapter.

> The moment you step out of context, you step onto the gerbil wheel of worship, relevance, and numbers

THE LAW OF DEVELOPMENT

Real Church Growth Is about Growing People, Not Managing Programs

Richard Kannwischer, the senior pastor of Peachtree Church in Atlanta, is a proud dog owner. One time Rich started training Shasta, a mini Australian shepherd that he got his girls for Christmas. But he felt that he needed professional help to go the rest of the way, so he hired a dog trainer.

When the trainer came to Rich's house, Rich wanted to get him up to speed on Shasta's progress. So Rich demonstrated for the trainer what he was already able to get his dog to do—sit, roll over, and so on. After the demonstration, Rich expected the trainer to give him an attaboy for his amateur dog training prowess, but he was disappointed. Instead, the trainer deflated him. "Your dog is not trained," the trainer said. "He just knows a few tricks."

Training versus Trying versus Tricks

When Rich absorbed what the dog trainer told him, a light bulb turned on in his mind. He wondered if something similar could be said of millions of Jesus followers in churches across North America: *your attenders are not trained; they just know a few church tricks.* They know how to sing along with the songs on Sunday morning. They know how to pray out loud with holy talk that everyone else uses. They know how to interact in a small group study. They might know how to give an acceptable percentage of their income. But does that mean they display automatic responses in the way of Jesus in their daily lives? More importantly, how would Rich tell the difference?

Years ago I remember John Ortberg getting at the dilemma in a somewhat different way by contrasting training and trying. Want to run a marathon? You can train or you can try. Without any training a person can muster their gusto and run headlong into breathless collapse on the side of the road. At mile fourteen, they simply cannot go farther in the marathon by sheer willpower. The body pushes back!

This applies to everything human beings do. Do you want to master the piano? You can train or you can try. Want to follow Jesus? You can train or you can try. You simply can't try your way into running a marathon or becoming a fine pianist. Doing these things takes discipline, repetition, progression, modeling, practice, evaluation, and accountability. Likewise, you can't try your way into a life that reflects the character and competencies of Jesus.

Program Church is sneaky. Ortberg's training-versus-trying contrast, brilliant as it is, does not sufficiently illuminate the stealthy way that Program Church influences what we have come to expect. That's why I like the revelation of Rich's dog trainer. The difference between training and succeeding on the one hand and trying and failing on the other is obvious, but that is not the more powerful trap. We get caught more easily in the self-deception of knowing a few tricks. Rich's dog didn't appear stuck in his stunts; he appeared adorably successful with his fun repetitive feats. Likewise, the deceptive power of Program Church does not give itself away in pointless trying but masks a failure of training with attendance success. We go through the program motions as if something real is happening. People learn just enough devotional devices and Jesus put-ons to offer false validation that a deeper, relational, maturing work of God is happening.

Rich Kannwischer's reflection is his own version of the challenge voiced by the two pastors at the beginning of this book. This chapter attempts to help leaders find answers by examining how disciple development in Future Church works differently from the customs of Program Church.

Programs Don't Develop People—People Do

The key words in the Program Church development strategy are *programs, addition,* and *teaching*. In Future Church these three still exist, but they fit in a broader framework whose key words are *people, multiplication,* and *training*.

First, in Program Church *programs* are made to develop people, but in Future Church programs are places where *people* develop people. In his classic book *The Master Plan of Evangelism,* Robert Coleman summarized Jesus's ministry strategy with an explosive four-word phrase: "Men were His method."[1] Jesus's playbook is and always will be people, not programs. "When the Lord is at work, you don't need heavy programs," Ray Ortlund says. "When the Lord isn't at work, you probably have to fake it."[2]

Discipleship programs can be valuable environments where development happens, but the program does not do the developing. Anytime a disciple truly grows in a program it is because there is a leader relationally tied to them actively guiding them along the path, a person whose life they want to emulate. In Future Church, programs are not the *what* but a *where* of disciple making.

This distinction is important because of what Jesus said about a student becoming like their teacher. When a person develops a disciple, the disciple grows into a person who develops disciples. But when a program develops a disciple, the disciple grows into a person who services programs. It is like the difference between growing a queen bee that gives birth to new life and growing a worker bee that lives to maintain the hive.

The difference between a queen bee and a worker bee brings us to the second contrast between *addition* and *multiplication*. When programs are done well, they can serve increasing numbers of people. This is certainly better than subtraction, but it is not enough for the mission God designed and deploys. The first command God gave Adam and Eve in Genesis is to multiply; our biology informs our ecclesiology and our missiology. The × is more important than the + on a kingdom calculator. Jesus's method is not to add people one at a time at a steady rate. It is to impart his own life to multiple people who each would impart it to multiple others. Set against the backdrop of a global population of 7,768,734,372 at the time of this writing, addition strategies are just a drop in the bucket. We simply will not reach billions of people in danger of eternal judgment without multiplication. We were made to reproduce, not recruit.

We were made to reproduce, not recruit.

This multiplication principle is well known among church leaders but not well applied. As I described in part 1, when multiplication starts at the level of launching worship services, new campus sites, or even churches, it often skips the basic, personal level of disciples multiplying disciples. The result is the apparent multiplication of God's work, but in reality it is a program addition equivalent to a house of cards: new believers are not developed as much as existing believers are reshuffled into new places in the deck.

One reason that multiplication is limited in churches is that when they add programs to help people grow, these are generally for *teaching*, not *training*. Do not misunderstand: teaching programs have a rich and worthy basis. Jesus was a teacher, as were the apostles, and the New Testament is full of their teaching.

Teaching and teachers are among the spiritual gifts that the Lord gave his church.

But not all teaching helps people be "doers of the word and not hearers only" (James 1:22 ESV). It is also not how people are educated for practical action in other fields. For instance, you don't teach someone to swim in a classroom. You don't explain the fundamental principles of swimming and share inspirational stories of swimmers and then expect people to go off on their own and swim laps that week. You teach people to swim by getting into a pool with them.

Preaching and teaching in a large gathering do have value that I will define in this chapter. But you don't teach people to swim or play piano or fix a leaky faucet or do algebra or follow Jesus by telling them. You do it by showing them, coaching them, and giving them something to practice—in short, by training them.

What a Tire and a Basement Teach about Development

Admittedly, the notion of training disciples can be rather intimidating to many church leaders, because it is difficult to train a disciple when you have not been trained yourself. Some of us were taught to train believers. Many of us were trained to teach them. But few of us were intentionally trained to train them.

But there is no need to fear. I am confident that you already know everything about development that you need to know. You may simply not know that you know it.

When I was consulting with Bellevue Baptist Church in Memphis and talking with its leadership team about developing disciples, I asked them to tell me about a time that they learned a skill outside of church. One leader in his late sixties told me about how he learned to sell tires in his first job in high school. He had spent a career buying and selling car dealerships, but half a century later he could still tell me in step-by-step detail how to sell a tire. I had no doubt that even after all that time he could walk out of the church at that moment and sell a set of tires to a customer without batting an eye. That is what genuine development looks like.

It is crucial to recognize that development is everywhere. When I say that the mission Jesus gave us is to make disciples, I do not mean that we are turning people who are not disciples into people who are. Rather, we are turning people into disciples of Jesus who have been disciples of someone or something else their whole lives. They may not be conscious, intentional, deliberate disciples, but they are disciples all the same. They are learning a way to live from the world around them. Christian disciple making is nothing other than winning people from their default teachers to the superior Teacher and instructing them to obey everything he commanded us.[3]

In 1983, Buddy and Jody Hoffman planted Grace Fellowship Church on this principle in a suburb of Atlanta. For Buddy and Jody, disciple making happened in the world and on the job, not just in a classroom or a small group.[4]

When several leaders came on staff at Grace, Buddy and Jody invited them to live together in their basement. They interacted with Buddy and Jody in their real lives. The leaders tagged along when Buddy was ministering, and he gave them real ministry assignments of their own. The basement became a training greenhouse for learning and evaluation in ways that a thousand programs could never replicate. Buddy and Jody provided similar access even to those who were not living in the basement. As a result, a group of leaders developed in the way of Jesus, which affected not only their official ministry assignments but also how they saw and viewed everything.

Several years later, Buddy went down with an unexpected aortic dissection that almost cost him his life, yet these leaders rose up in his absence. By this time Grace had planted a few campuses beyond the original site, which were each led by a leader he had trained. Once Buddy recovered, he returned as pastor but not in the same way. Instead of going back to pastor the mother church, he chose to operate on the edges of the movement, planting two more campuses himself before he died. This began to move Grace from being a large megachurch with a few campuses to becoming a multiplying family of churches.

More significantly, however, Buddy's basement produced not only leaders—many of whom are still leading churches in the Grace network—but a method of ministry and people development that has continued long after his death. Throughout the Grace Family of Churches, the basement continues to function. Sometimes it is still actual basements that house young leaders on staff. Other times the basements are training initiatives like 10,000 Fathers for worship leaders and preachers. In still other cases the basements are training centers in churches for ordinary disciples.

At a recent meeting, Grace's senior pastors discussed their capacity for planting churches, arriving at this conclusion: "We are not very good at planting churches. But we are good at raising leaders who succeed in planting churches despite how bad we are at planting churches." This is what happens when a church embraces the Upper Room Law of Development—when it puts growing people ahead of managing programs.

Three Areas of Development

For us to invest in growing people and escape the trap of program management, we need to consider a bit more deeply why we tend to fall into the program rut. One reason that programs are popular is that leaders have not always thought carefully about what to pass on to people to encourage their development. By looking at three areas in which a disciple needs to develop (in addition to personal character, which is its own topic), we can see why programs alone never get it done.[5]

Doctrinal Development

The first area usually considered when developing a disciple is doctrine. Here I use the term "doctrine" expansively to include any facts or ideas that are worthwhile for a Jesus follower to know and believe—not only basic theology but also the content of books of the Bible, moral principles, even Christian history. Doctrinal teaching does not have to be dry. As Howard Hendriks used to say, "It's a sin to bore people with the Bible." But knowledge transfer is the point.

The most important thing to understand about doctrine is that it is the dimension of development that is easiest to program. First, doctrinal development is labor-efficient. One person can convey it to thousands at once—or through books, audio, and video, even to millions more at the learner's own time, pace, and place. Second, doctrinal development requires no relationship between the teacher and the learners; they can be strangers to each other. Third, doctrinal development can be formally structured in an orderly sequence that does not need to respond to changing circumstances. In fact, following a logical progression may make it most effective. All these features of doctrine respond very well to an organized program.

Here is the key takeaway for ministry strategy: *because doctrinal development is easiest to program, it usually gets programmed everywhere.* Obviously, the preaching event is a good vehicle for doctrinal development, but information transfer dominates most small groups as well. Think about it: a group streams a video of a teacher from some big church somewhere and reads the book that teacher wrote. They then discuss its ideas, which is a helpful follow-up to make doctrine absorption sink in deeper. Finally (ideally) they share prayer requests and have supportive social time together, which, while beautiful and essential, frequently has little developmental value. The small group accomplishes the same thing as the big group but with less music and more conversation (and maybe dessert).

Doctrinal development is very important; we should have more of it, not less. But it does not train someone to live as a follower of Jesus. A person can hear many sermons, attend many small groups, and absorb many ideas and not appreciably change in any area but their knowledge base. A sermon may (and should) *inspire* action, but without something more it does not *impel* action. It might get listeners as far as appreciation, but by itself it does not get them to transformation. As Jesus said in one of his own sermons (a better message than any we have ever preached), "Why do you call me, 'Lord, Lord,' and do not do what I say?" (Luke 6:46).

Skills Development

We move into the realm of training when we look at another area of development that churches often overlook—skills.

Disciples of Jesus do certain things simply because they are disciples of Jesus. Disciples pray for a variety of reasons and in diverse settings. Disciples worship God weekly with other disciples. Disciples pitch in to help out each other, their neighbors, and their church. Disciples read the Bible daily for knowledge and for insight. Disciples listen to hurting people and express compassion. Disciples give their material wealth for the relief of those who do not have it and for the spread of the gospel. Disciples reconcile with each other when one has hurt another. The list could go on.

Nobody is born knowing how to do these things practically. These are skills that must be learned. To convey skills to disciples effectively, we have to go about it in a different way than we go about doctrinal development. First, even though efficient one-to-many resources can be helpful, a person rarely masters a skill just by reading a book or watching a video. Skills development usually requires intensive coaching from one trainer to a few apprentices.

Second, a person can learn doctrine from someone they have never met, but skills development requires a moderately close relationship. The discipler and disciples may not have to divulge their deepest secrets or allow access into all areas of their lives, but they do need to get to know each other personally and honestly and have good rapport over a long term for skills to pass from one to the next.

Third, as with doctrine, skills development often has some degree of formal structure (learning things step-by-step in a prescribed order or method). But there is a large *situational* element too. If a disciple has trouble acquiring a skill, the discipler follows up one-on-one. Or sometimes an urgent situation means that a new skill needs to be learned right away.

To train a disciple to develop a skill, the key is to reverse engineer how you learned it yourself. Recalling the businessman at Bellevue, I had him walk back through the process of selling a tire. If you do this with the development of any skill, you will always see four basic ingredients: modeling, practice, evaluation, and accountability in the setting of a relationship.

- *Modeling*—the discipler demonstrates the skill in its typical place of application with the disciple watching
- *Practice*—the disciple tries to perform the skill repeatedly, sometimes first in a laboratory setting with the discipler's coaching
- *Evaluation*—the disciple demonstrates the skill in its typical place of application with the discipler watching to praise and encourage and to note areas of improvement
- *Accountability*—there is an expectation of consistent participation and activity; absenteeism and unpreparedness are called out

Skills are (almost) the most neglected area of Christian development. The average church spends little time investing in it. Churches driven by worship, relevance, and numbers are virtually allergic to modeling, practice, evaluation, and accountability (at least outside the staff) because they scare some people off. But if you are going to engage in organized disciple making, you eventually have to do what Jesus did: look for learners in the crowd of consumers and give them your best.

One way I have attempted to fill the void of discipleship skills development is by partnering with Dave Rhodes to start a company called Younique. Younique equips churches to train every believer in the skills of gospel-centered life design—how to find their calling in life and live it out God's way. Younique is unlike much of what a person encounters in church. It is not primarily knowledge transfer like a Bible study, though it does communicate biblical principles. It is not primarily character formation, though it requires self-examination and often catalyzes inner development. Rather, Younique primarily trains people in the skills of living out their special assignment from God in all of life.

Another venue of skills development is leadership development. Many churches, struggling to win volunteer hours from busy people, see this as their pressing need. But how to equip leaders to succeed remains a mystery to many. The best many do is doctrinal knowledge transfer: "Congratulations on becoming an elder; here's a systematic theology for you to read."

By contrast, my good friend and leadership development maven Mac Lake insists that in addition to content about Jesus and the character of Jesus, leaders need to grow in the competence of Jesus. To that end, Mac has pioneered competency-focused leadership development content for the church. This kind of material does not attempt to cultivate leadership proficiency by mere reading or open-ended talking. Instead, it combines reading Scripture and leadership content with practical assignments tailored to the core competencies of a given leadership role. Most importantly, it is not a self-directed course of training; rather, it is explicitly built for a personal coaching relationship between an experienced leader and a trainee. In short, the curriculum goes beyond knowledge transfer to modeling, practice, evaluation, and accountability.[6]

Reproductive Development

In rare instances that church leaders delineate the skills that are important for every Christian to have, they usually list something like sharing one's faith. That makes sense. Telling one's personal story of salvation and articulating the gospel to ask for a response are certainly skills to be learned. But I actually think they belong in a different category.

Think of it this way. In order to become a mature, self-sufficient adult, you needed to master a variety of skills. But if you became a parent, you had to learn a whole other set of skills that is a level beyond the skills you require for your own survival. Growing up to maturity is one thing; raising someone else to maturity is another matter.

Reproductive development, like skills development, happens in a smaller circle with shorter distance between teacher and learners than doctrinal development does. The relationship is more intimate than skills development, and the structure is even more spontaneous, responding to situations in the person's life. In all respects, reproduction happens up close and personal.

> Growing up to maturity is one thing; raising someone else to maturity is another matter.

The Law of Development states that real church growth is about growing people, not adding programs. Reproduction is the reason why. When you see clearly what reproduction entails, you understand why programs cannot generate it any more than a factory can bear and raise a child. Programs and preaching are helps for spiritual parenting, but they are not spiritual parents. By themselves, at their best, programs and preaching yield people who invite others to programs and preaching. They do not produce reproducers. But producing reproducers is what disciple making is all about.

In the Great Commission (Matt. 28:18–20), Jesus tells his disciples to make disciples. He says that this includes "teaching them to obey everything" that Jesus commanded *his* disciples, *including the Great Commission*. Therefore, if you would obey the Great Commission, you have not succeeded until you have also taught someone else to obey all Jesus's commands, including the Great

Commission. In other words, you have not obeyed the Great Commission until the disciple you make also makes a disciple—*until you have reproduced a reproducer.*

The church is nothing other than the group of people among whom this is happening. The services, the songs, and the sermons; the budgets, the buildings, and the boards; even the good deeds—everything in the church that holds most leaders' attention most of the time—are not church unless they are usefully helping ordinary disciples who are reproducing Christ in others. In C. S. Lewis's memorable words, "The Church exists for nothing else but to draw men into Christ, to make them little Christs. If they are not doing that, all the cathedrals, clergy, missions, sermons, even the Bible itself, are simply a waste of time."[7]

Revolutionary Coaching

A pastor named Mark was a professional tennis coach in his earlier days. When Mark would be approached by a new client, he would ask the person one question at the outset: "Do you want to improve your weekend game, or do you want to win a tournament?"

The question was important because it set the guidelines of instruction. If the goal was improving the player's weekend game, the method was *evolutionary*: tweaking what the player was already doing and adding some new techniques. But if the goal was winning a tournament, the method was *revolutionary*: forcing the player to unlearn their technique and starting over from the beginning.

When Jesus coaches us, he is not about minor improvements; he is about winning the tournament. He wants the Holy Spirit to radically rearrange a person's responses to everything that happens in their life so that they respond like he would. This revolutionary change does not happen by itself in a big group or even a small group a few times a month. It happens in the intimate spaces and practical proving grounds at all times of day.

Jesus knew that most people who liked listening to him were not ready for this level of coaching. That is why he said things like:

- "Small is the gate and narrow the road that leads to life, and only a few find it" (Matt. 7:14).
- "Many are invited, but few are chosen" (Matt. 22:14).
- "Those of you who do not give up everything you have cannot be my disciples" (Luke 14:33).

Seekers have the virtue of fortitude—persevering courage. Seekers take initiative. Seekers want to be trained, not just try or learn a few tricks. "Seeker" should not be a label just for people who are not disciples of Jesus yet; all true disciples are seekers who never stop seeking. Fortitude is what makes them "press on toward the goal for the prize of the upward call of God in Christ Jesus" (Phil. 3:14 ESV).

On the other side of the coin, leaders who are making disciples need fortitude as well. They need persevering courage to concentrate their energies on making disciples when there are many distractions of the good that can divert them from the great. There are people who would actually prefer to learn a few tricks to being fully trained, people who prefer programs that meet their needs as conveniently as possible. There are even professional rewards for managing programs over growing people, not to mention that it always feels good to see more people show up.

Yet leaders in Future Church have the fortitude to prioritize the seekers that Jesus prioritized, even when the crowd of consumers presents distractions. They don't settle for immediate results that come by managing programs but instead give themselves to an unbroken chain of people helping people grow over the long haul. That's real church growth.

THE LAW OF LEADERSHIP

Real Church Growth Is Led by Calling, Not Celebrity

Over the career I have led as a consultant, I have met so many interesting pastors that it would be impossible for me to pick favorites. But two stick out for similar reasons: Chuck Swindoll and Max Lucado.

I worked with Chuck's team at Stonebriar Community Church in the Dallas area when I was in my early thirties and with Max's at Oak Hills Church in San Antonio in my late thirties. As with all my clients, I began my on-site work by attending weekend worship incognito, much the same way that retail corporations hire mystery shoppers. As a secret worshiper at Stonebriar and Oak Hills, I saw something I have never seen anywhere else: chartered coach buses full of believers from other cities who traveled to hear the famous preachers.

I admit I was impressed. These worshipers were drawn by the awesomely gifted communication of two celebrity pastors, and I was pretty starstruck myself. The chartered buses stroked my own ego; the tourists they carried validated me as a consultant because I now had popular personalities for clients.

What made Chuck and Max unforgettable clients, however, was that they were not nearly as impressed by their celebrity status as I was. A couple stories bear this out.

The first one is that in all my years as a consultant, I have only worked with one pastor who took initiative to learn my children's names and prayed for them individually when he said grace over lunch. That pastor is Max Lucado. Max's love for children is well known through his children's books and videos, and I can attest that it is as genuine as any quality I have ever seen in a person.

The second story comes from my consulting at Stonebriar. When I compared a year's adult baptisms to worship attendance, I discovered that it took over four hundred adults at Stonebriar one year to make one new adult follower of Jesus. When I presented this statistic to the church's senior leadership, Chuck Swindoll— mega-successful church planter and the president of my seminary when I was a student—asked, "Will, what does this mean?"

I replied, "Chuck, it means that as a family of believers, Stonebriar is impotent as a church." (I'm a bit more diplomatic now than I was then.)

Chuck could have gotten defensive. He could have gotten angry. He could have said, "Who do you think you are, you little punk?" But he did the complete opposite. He listened. He learned. He thought deeply about the changes needed to be a more evangelistically effective church. He wanted Stonebriar to be more than a personality-driven Lower Room. Like Max Lucado, he never wanted his face to be a part of the church's brand and he didn't want to draw attention to himself. Despite their celebrity status, both of these men demonstrated unusual humility and teachability.

Unfortunately, there are pastors and churches far more attached to celebrity than Chuck and Stonebriar and Max and Oak Hills are. Celebrity is not sin, but it is a dangerous source of temptation. Concerningly, celebrity is bolted into the ministry models of churches of all sizes, because it naturally goes together with a culture of worship, the power of relevance, the validation of numbers, and the importation of growth. Yet celebrity is the counterfeit of leadership.

The Green Room Syndrome

When Mike Breen came from the United Kingdom to the United States to launch 3DMovements (3DM), he brought insightful disciple-making tools with him. One tool that has been adapted through the ministry of Younique is LifeDrifts, based on Jesus's temptation by Satan in Luke 4:1–11. The LifeDrifts summarize all temptation and sin in three broad categories: *appetite, ambition,* and *approval.* These simple categories are extremely helpful for personal spiritual formation.

In the desert, Jesus was tempted to turn stone into bread, the temptation of appetite (becoming one's own provider rather than trusting God to provide); to gain authority over all kingdoms by worshiping the devil, the temptation of ambition (justifying legitimate ends by any means necessary); and to leap off the roof of the temple in view of the people below, the temptation of approval (using a valid identity to create a selfish spectacle).[1] These three drifts summarize every human being's impulse to have more (appetite), to accomplish more (ambition), and to be more (approval).

In addition, however, these three LifeDrifts also reveal the temptations that entice organizations—we might call them ChurchDrifts. With an outsider's perspective, Breen saw how the drifts of appetite, ambition, and approval were the invisible, subversive drivers of the North American church:

- Appetite is evidenced in the church when discipleship is replaced by *consumerism*—never an overt intention in preaching but a powerful motivational undercurrent in the social contract between good church members and good church pastors.

- Ambition is evidenced when mission is distracted by *competition*—not an explicit strategy to compete with other churches but a passive willingness to see transfer growth as an acceptable validation of successful mission.
- Approval is evidenced in the church when biblical leadership is replaced by *celebrity*—not by the obvious evil of egomaniacal pastors but by the apparent good of heroes craved by American popular culture.[2]

When we say celebrity replaces leadership, we mean that when someone is good at drawing attention and inspiring the masses, people automatically ascribe authority to that individual whether or not the person has true spiritual authority. The assumption is that the most compelling communicator is the most worthy leader. Disciple-faking success is associated with a big physical platform (worship attendance) combined with a big virtual platform (social media impressions) that yields a big publishing platform (books, studies, e-courses) that all combine to make a big marketing platform for the celebrity's personal brand.

As with the other laws, this is not the problem of the megachurch only. My coauthor Cory Hartman told me about a time he attended a weekend worship service at a church plant meeting in a converted commercial space near his home. This church had the formula down pat. There was a platoon of well-trained guest experience specialists, a welcome center with branded coffee mugs, and a corner of the room reserved for the bookstore with titles by big-platform preachers. At worship time there was a totally dark house, a blazingly lit stage, a guy and a gal giving announcements with the polish of morning talk show hosts, and a guitar-playing lead vocalist in thick-rimmed glasses, skinny jeans, a graphic tee, and a scarf, singing in keys no one else could sing along with.

The church had good signage too. The thing that cracked Cory up was a door at house right marked "Green Room." *A green room?* Who did the speaker need to hide from to prepare himself? There were only fifty people in the building! Did he think he would be overwhelmed by the throngs desperate to get his attention if he sat with everyone else?

Nevertheless, you don't have to have a green room to get caught in the green room syndrome. While the North American context equates skills in communicating from a platform with leadership skills, that's not the exclusive problem with celebrity—not even the most important one. Even when a great communicator is also a great leader, the dynamic of celebrity wreaks havoc, because celebrity reinforces all the other problems of fake church growth and violates the Seven Laws of the Upper Room. It concentrates the culture on worship services instead of mission (Law 1). It often entices attenders and leaders with the allure of relevance, not the gospel (Law 2). It is validated by numbers, not unity (Law 3). It grows by importing people, not by local context (Law 4). It adds programs that project the celebrity's output instead of multiplying people by life-on-life disciple making (Law 5). And as we will see in the next chapter, it models the false narratives of people's natural preferences over the true narrative of kingdom imagination (Law 7). Ultimately, celebrity undermines the calling of each individual, whether leaders or followers.

Celebrity and Authority in Jesus's Leadership

Despite these tough words against celebrity, I sincerely feel for pastors who don't want to be celebrities themselves but feel pressure to become one. The reality is that without being conscious of it, many people in churches *want* a celebrity pastor. They flock to the churches where a celebrity already occupies the platform, or else they hope or even actively encourage their pastor to become one.

In fact, celebrities have been part of the Christian church throughout its history. Although celebrity is a dangerous problem for the church, celebrities themselves can be faithful servants of God. We know this because we have the example of a model celebrity to follow: the Lord Jesus himself.

Jesus was a huge celebrity, but celebrity had nothing to do with his leadership. His leadership was about calling. He was called by God to do a job: "The Spirit of the Lord is on me, because he has anointed me to proclaim good news to the poor" (Luke 4:18). Importantly, with his calling came authority: what God called him to do, God gave him authority to do. Jesus's leadership was not derived from his celebrity, which comes from people. His leadership came from his authority, which comes from God, who has all authority.

Once we grasp that Jesus's leadership was derived from his authority, we can understand why he was so unattached to celebrity. He had no problem drawing attention to himself when the time was right—for example, when he entered Jerusalem for the Passover or when he overturned the tables of the money changers. Yet he also had no problem telling people he healed not to tell anyone what happened or making statements so confusing and outrageous that they drove people away. Celebrity was a tool he would employ or not employ according to the need of the moment, but it was not essential to himself or his leadership.

Shared Authority

Celebrity comes from people and authority comes from God, but that is not the only difference between them. The other difference is that celebrity cannot be shared, but authority can.

Celebrity is a zero-sum game. There are only so many eyes and ears in the world and only so many seconds per year for people to use them. So if people start paying more attention to you, they are paying less attention to others, maybe including me. If leadership is based on celebrity, then I must hold on to as much attention as possible, and I must be very sparing in how much I allow anyone else to receive. Otherwise, as the attention on me declines, my leadership effectiveness declines too. So, for example, if I control the platform or pulpit in a church, I must be strict with how many Sundays I give to subordinates to preach so that their celebrity does not eclipse mine.

Authority, on the other hand, is not a zero-sum game. Authority can multiply; it can be given without being given away. For instance, if you have the authority to write a check that draws money from a bank account, you can give someone else the authority to write a check on your behalf without losing any of your own authority to do it. In fact, their authority to write a check is based on yours.

This is the same way that authority worked in Jesus's leadership. When we explored the Law of Mission, we examined Luke's description of how Jesus gave authority to the twelve disciples and then to seventy-two others. Matthew's account of the same process straddles a break between chapters, so it is easy for us to miss the genius of what is really one continuous statement:

> Jesus *went through all the towns and villages, teaching in their synagogues, proclaiming the good news of the kingdom and healing every disease and sickness.* When he saw the crowds, he had compassion on them, because they were harassed and helpless, like sheep without a shepherd. Then he said to his disciples, "The harvest is plentiful but the workers are few. Ask the Lord of the harvest, therefore, to send out workers into his harvest field."
>
> Jesus called his twelve disciples to him and gave them authority to drive out impure spirits and to heal every disease and sickness. . . . "As you go, proclaim this message: 'The kingdom of heaven has come near.'" (Matt. 9:35–10:1, 7, emphasis added)

This passage is a sandwich.[3] It starts and ends the same way, with the explicit statement of mission—to proclaim the kingdom and to heal. In the middle of the sandwich we see the boundless compassion of Jesus colliding with the bottomless opportunity of mission, namely the "harassed and helpless" crowds. That missional motive in the heart of our Savior propels him to give away his authority to others—not a special group of celebrities but an unexpected band of amateurs. Faced with the size and scope of the task, Jesus refuses to be the solo minister. The repetition of the mission a second time in the text is significant: it amplifies the expansion of the mission through Jesus's delegation to others, not as mere volunteers but as empowered envoys. What Jesus did by the authority of the Father is what the Twelve do by the authority of Jesus.

> Faced with the size and scope of the task, Jesus refuses to be the solo minister.

When we read "authority," it is easy for us to interpret it as power; we think that Jesus gave the disciples supernatural power over disease and demons. Yet that is not the only understanding of authority and may not be the best one. Giving authority is also *giving permission*: Jesus's disciples had the *right* to preach the kingdom and heal people and cast out demons because Jesus gave them that right. They were *authorized*. This is what it means to speak, heal, act, and pray "in the name of Jesus": it means that you can do what you do because Jesus bestowed on you his own right to do it, which he received from the Father as his beloved Son.

This puts the Great Commission in a new light. Jesus begins that famous passage by reminding his disciples that "all authority in heaven and on earth has been given to me" by God (Matt. 28:18). On that basis, he grants his disciples the authority—the permission, the right, the prerogative—to make disciples. He concludes that he would be with them always: they would bear the flag of Jesus's kingdom as official ambassadors until the end of the age (v. 20).

Here we begin to recognize how dangerous Jesus is and what risks he is willing to take. Giving his authority to the Twelve is

scandalous by today's standards of ministry excellence considering the gap between their skill and Jesus's capacity, not to mention the gap in character. It is true that Jesus shared his authority
with men who had watched him carefully and who were being
trained. But it is not altogether clear whether these men had yet
"crossed over from death to life" when he first sent them out (John
5:24). Jesus gave authority to cast out demons to Judas Iscariot,
who soon would be invaded by Satan himself (Luke 22:3). Jesus
foresaw that at the last judgment he would tell some people who
worked miracles by his authority that he never knew them (Matt.
7:21–23). In fact, some people operated by his authority whom
he literally did not know personally, such as the man casting out
demons in his name who did not follow along with Jesus's gang
of disciples (Luke 9:49–50).

The astonishing kicker is that Jesus did not only share his authority with the Twelve; he has shared his authority *with us*. He
went away and gave us his Holy Spirit, a worldwide mission, and
his authority to carry it out, and he seems to think that is enough
for us to handle it.

Are you beginning to see the difference between leading by
celebrity and leading by authority? In churches large and small,
the powers that be are careful not to give too much influence, control, and access to people for fear they will compromise their own
influence or maybe the excellence of the program. They mistake
the expandable pie of authority for a more-for-you-means-less-
for-me slice of celebrity.

I cannot overstate how much this posture compromises the
mission of Jesus every day. When God came to earth and modeled effective leadership, he empowered others at light speed. He
quickly gave the ball away, creating a team of quarterbacks, running backs, and wide receivers who score kingdom touchdowns.
But when the average pastor steps into their calling, they are likely
to lead like the ball hog on the third grade playground—and not
just for one season but for the entirety of their ministry.

What would happen in your ministry if you instead declared amateur hour just like Jesus does? He shares his kingdom authority far and wide with people like us who are embarrassingly unqualified at first blush but are made adequate by him (2 Cor. 3:6). He gives his kids the keys to the Corvette with all the risks of what might happen when they peel out of the driveway.

We have been conditioned to believe that those with the greatest impact are those with the biggest platform. Yet Jesus had that platform and could have made it even bigger, but he spurned the opportunity. While other rabbis then and teachers now build a platform, Jesus built a pipeline, and his impact was inconceivably greater. He shared his leadership to multiply leaders. His calling was to give away a calling.

Everyone Is Called

As we have seen, one problem with leadership-by-celebrity is that it fails to recognize the authority that Jesus has given to all his disciples. That authority is part of the general calling that God issues to all believers to be saved and to serve. In addition, however, celebrity also fails to recognize the special calling that God has given to each individual believer.

In Ephesians 2:10, Paul writes that "we are God's handiwork, created in Christ Jesus to do good works, which God prepared in advance for us to do." We can certainly name general good works that God intended for all his redeemed people to do, chief among them to love him with our whole being and to love our neighbors as ourselves. But Paul's sentence hints at something much more specific than that. It says that God *prepared* good works for us to do. Since the beginning of time God has been cooking up a special recipe of particular impact where you live, work, and play every day.

The word "prepared" is not the only clue that you have a special assignment from God. There is also the word "handiwork."

When God sculpted you, was he less than Michelangelo? When God penned the drama of your story-script, was he less than Shakespeare? A mere glance at this wonder-filled world reminds us that we are products of mind-blowing mastery. If we are his handiwork, he must have uniquely crafted each of us by the delicate tools of nature and nurture, high points and hard times. If God prepared good works in advance for you to do, he must have prepared you to do them. He must have designed you in a particular way for a set of particular days, the moments when you show off Christ as a one-of-a-kind display.

No one else can do what God prepared for you to do. You have an ultimate contribution to make and a legacy to leave with your life. It will never happen unless you walk in the works he prepared in advance for you, starting now.

This is a truly awesome thought. But its corollary is just as important: *everyone else in Christ is God's handiwork too.* That's right: these lofty truths are not only true of you but are also true of every single believer in your church. Every. Single. One. Therefore, even though God has placed you in your church as a leader, there are others in the church whom, according to their gifting and their faith, he expects you to follow.

When celebrity thrives in the church, it tends to choke out each believer's special calling like the kudzu of the kingdom. Kudzu is the invasive plant species that grows along roadsides in the Southeastern US, smothering other plants and trees under a leafy blanket. It can spread at the extremely rapid pace of one foot per day. It hogs the sunlight like celebrities hog the limelight, leaving other life under its shadow to wither and eventually die.[4] Churches might readily affirm the gifts of individuals in the worship center, but in practice those strengths are lost in the glare of the spotlight on one. Celebrity monopolizes calling. Pastors stay heroes, never to become hero makers.

Leaders who pursue celebrity usually have a fertile imagination for the specific contribution to the kingdom God wants them to make in their lifetime. But they tend to lack imagination for the ultimate contributions of others. While they would never consciously think it, they operate with an assumption that *"your* calling is to watch me work *my* calling."

While working on this chapter I got a text from a friend, a brilliant thinker, a megachurch elder, and a passionate disciple maker. Not long ago he scored a contract with a major Christian publisher for a book on how to apply innovation in the church, yet for months he felt like he could not share the news with the handful of full-time pastors at his church. After he eventually informed the pastoral team, I inquired about their response. He told me that they didn't say much; he figured they don't have the time. This situation breaks my heart. When an everyday elder has been given a chance to have a national voice, his pastors not only failed to celebrate, but they hardly acknowledged his contribution.

In celebrity-based leadership, fame is retained, not retrained. It's the exact opposite of disciple making, in which "everyone who is fully trained will be like their teacher" (Luke 6:40). By contrast, calling-based leadership sees no tension or competition between the discipler's calling and the disciple's. The discipler coaches the disciple into how Jesus would live if he were that person.

In celebrity-based leadership, fame is retained, not retrained.

Whether the disciple's special calling ultimately garners more attention or less than the discipler's is irrelevant.

The Pastorhood of Every Believer

Churches can take steps to reduce their reliance on celebrity, many of which have to do with optics; for example, don't get caught on social media wearing $600 sneakers. But such advice does not benefit the vast majority of church leaders, for whom trappings of celebrity are not realistic.

Even though image-management advice may be necessary for some pastors, it is still a surface-level way to deal with the problem. It is less important for leadership that we tamp down celebrity than that we lift up calling; that is the priority of the Upper Room. To that end, here are two shifts we will see in Future Church.

Leader Shift #1: Call Every Believer to Engage Their Parish

One of the game-changing propositions of the Protestant Reformation was the idea of "the priesthood of all believers." This slogan summarized the Bible's teaching that "there is one God and one mediator between God and mankind, the man Christ Jesus, who gave himself as a ransom for all people" (1 Tim. 2:5–6). He is the only go-between we have with God; we have no other priest.

However, because Jesus is the great High Priest (Heb. 4:14), all of us have been redeemed to become priests ourselves: we are "a holy priesthood, offering spiritual sacrifices acceptable to God through Jesus Christ" (1 Pet. 2:5). The priesthood of all believers means that everyone has a role to play serving God. No one has superior status over another by virtue of their church position.

As Protestants, it is easy for us to nod in agreement with these ideas. But that is because, unless we are Anglicans or Episcopalians, we do not call our professional church leaders priests. We call them pastors. So we miss the shocking power of the slogan as it sounded in Reformation Europe. "The priesthood of all believers" sounded to them like "the *pastorhood* of all believers" sounds to us today.

Is that wording uncomfortable? Maybe so, but the Upper Room insists on the pastorhood of all believers. Every believer is a pastor who must declare their parish. Every believer has a crowd to serve the gospel to. Every believer must watch themselves and their teaching (1 Tim. 4:16). Every believer is charged with growing their flock in the faith of Christ. Every believer has authority from Jesus to baptize disciples and teach them everything he commanded (Matt. 28:19–20).

Leader Shift #2: Normalize the Reality of Vocational Ministry

In older lingo, "minister" was a word for a person who did pastoral work as a job or in an official capacity. Today that term is used less often because of the recognition that every believer is (or should be) a minister. Yet we still use "vocational ministry" to refer to a career serving churches.

This terminology is not an improvement, however. "Vocation" comes from the Latin word meaning "call"; along these lines, in many denominations one must enunciate one's call to ministry in order to be ordained.

But *every* believer has a call to ministry; *all* of us are called by God to serve, and each of us is called to serve in a unique way that no one else is. There may be such a thing as pastors who are compensated as full-time workers. There may be such a thing as pastors with an ordination or certification status as a result of their education. But in Future Church, these specifics are not equated with vocational ministry. Everyone called by the grace of God to serve him is considered a vocational minister.

Therefore, as calling becomes more prominent in Future Church, the lines between vocational, bivocational, covocational, and nonvocational ministry as we understand them today will fade both in our minds and also in our organizational structures. We will see churches with one or two full-time staff pastors increasingly replaced by churches with ten or twelve paid part-time overseers who work day jobs.

This shift will not just be a product of the gig economy or a tactic to trim the cost of employment benefits (though those will both be factors). It will also come because the number one qualification of elders/overseers will be their proficiency in making disciples. Future Church will abound with disciple making, so there will be plenty of qualified leaders. In addition, the church will begin to view so-called secular employment as an asset for its leaders, because it keeps them in touch with more people who need to meet Jesus. Leadership from the Upper Room will involve more marketplace missionaries than program priests.

What will tie each believer's diverse activities together—whether paid or unpaid—is a strong grasp of their one thing, their special calling from God that transcends and unifies all the different occupational boxes that make up their working life inside and outside the church. Their one thing, whatever it is, is their true vocation, their true call. (I expound on this more deeply in my book *Clarity Spiral: The 4 Break-Thru Practices to Find the One Thing You're Called to Do.*[5])

> *Read more about a third leader shift—new models of ministry education for all believers—at futurechurchbook.com/bonus.*

The Laity Are the Clergy

The word "clergy" and its related terms in other languages have been used to refer to a caste of church leaders for hundreds of years. Surprisingly, the word's origin is from the Greek word meaning "lot" or "allotment." It may come from the pattern of the Levitical priests who had no allotment of land in Israel because "the LORD is their inheritance" (Deut. 18:2). But it may also come from the idea that each elder/overseer had an allotted flock to watch over—the people God put into their hands.[6]

But in truth, all believers are given an allotment of people to serve the gospel to and raise to perfection in Christ, people God has placed all around them. Each of the "common people" has an allotment—the laity are the clergy.

In order to see and treat the people of God as the clergy that they are, leaders need to grow in the virtue of justice. The church will not rise as a mature body in Christ until all believers treat themselves and each other justly. Both leaders and those led must recognize that God, being just, shows no favoritism; he distributes talents to each of his servants to make the most of for his glory (Matt. 25:14–30). A just church is one where the highest calling of every leader is to see every disciple flourish in their own calling, because "God is no respecter of persons" (Acts 10:34 KJV).

The church invests considerable resources to recruit and resource church planters, as it should. But the day that every believer climbs the stairs to the Upper Room and realizes that they are a pastor with a flock God has allotted to them is the day that millions of new churches get planted all over North America. Those microchurches and the leaders called to them already exist; they are just waiting to be seen for what they are. That is real church growth.

12

THE LAW OF VISION

Real Church Growth Is Energized by Shared Imagination, Not Shared Preference

I started teaching my daughter Poema how to play billiards at the young age of two. I almost began by reaching for a junior-sized cue stick, but I realized that was a bit ambitious. We needed to start with the most basic idea: get the ball into the pocket!

So I pulled up a fluffy beanbag ottoman to make a comfy step stool. Now she could stand head and shoulders above the expansive table. Next I wanted to teach her to feel the win. I put a ball in her hand and showed her how to roll it into the side pocket. When she rolled one of the bright balls into the pocket I yelled, "Made it!" and spun around in a dramatic victory dance. When the ball missed and ricocheted off the cushion, my face drooped with a sad declaration, "Missed it!"

Through a systematic journey of daily pool lessons I guided my daughter in the way of billiard legends. But one thing kept getting in the way: her creativity. Unencumbered by the finite game of eight ball, her playful eyes invented new ways of viewing the colorful spheres on the tabletop.

The most important interruption occurred when her sensibilities as a budding ballet dancer collided with my training regimen.

One day she sent two balls spinning in close proximity to one another. The bright red three ball and yellow-striped nine ball spiraled in a waltz across the tan felt. To Poema, the billiard balls weren't hurtling for a side pocket score anymore; they were doing something much more marvelous. "Look, Dadda," she declared, "the balls are dancing!" Poema's eyes opened with delight—the pool table had become a dance hall.

With the patience only available to an older father, I smiled and paused the lesson. I learned that the pool table was a more creative place than I ever dreamed. Now I am practicing billiards dance moves that would make Willie Mosconi jealous. I was determined to teach Poema how to play pool, but she was determined to use her imagination.

It's not as though I wasn't using my own imagination at the pool table; it takes imagination to look at colored balls and see a game. But my imagination had hardened into assumption. Years of playing billiards highly refined what I saw when I stepped up to the table. I saw the boundaries of a finite game. I knew the rules, and I knew when I broke them. I knew how to score and how to win. When I started teaching Poema, I was operating out of paradigm lock—that was *all* I could see. It certainly was not a bad thing; there is a lot of fun playing in that paradigm. But a child showed me that it is not the only paradigm. It was helpful to me—refreshing even—to be reminded of my own one-dimensional perspective.

My game with Poema is an everyday illustration of what my friend Alan Hirsch discusses quite a bit with respect to the church: paradigm blindness. In their book *The Permanent Revolution*, Alan and coauthor Tim Catchim describe how a way of doing church creates a sort of theological amnesia. Shut in the predictable patterns of Program Church, we forget its core disciple-making DNA:

> We create a paradigm—a way of perceiving our world, of filtering out what is considered real and unreal, of creating mental models of how things should be. Once established, paradigms in many

ways do our thinking for us. . . . Although paradigms help us make sense of our world by giving us ways to interpret it, they also create what is called paradigm blindness: an incapacity to see things from outside that particular perspective or paradigm. . . . For instance, well-worn formulas are used to define what it is to be a church (referred to as the marks of the church). . . . And yet without some serious theological gymnastics, they are patently deficient, especially in making space for the tasks of mission, discipleship, and human community.[1]

Many church leaders have been playing by the rules of Program Church for a long time. Their sanctuaries and worship centers are their game tables. They know how to score—with butts in seats instead of billiard balls in pool table pockets—and they know who is winning and who is losing.

The paradigm lock of Program Church tees up the seventh law, the Law of Vision: *real church growth is energized by shared imagination, not shared preference.* Unlike the other laws, I have been thinking about this one every day for twenty years. Now I see it as the culminating principle of all the laws of the Upper Room.

What I am talking about is not a matter of mere excitement; all church leaders start out excited to do church. As we lead others, we naturally want to pass on our passion for the things of God. But what if our daily efforts to get people energized about church are being sabotaged by the Lower Room in ways that evade our awareness? What if the everyday church leader has access to a realm of human empowerment that we are not even close to utilizing? What if we have lobotomized the imaginative capacity of the body of Christ?

What if we have lobotomized the imaginative capacity of the body of Christ?

Leading from the Upper Room means energizing God's people with the creative capacity to see a better future. The mission of Jesus is the most imaginative endeavor on the planet, a game we play with God until Christ returns. As the Spirit of God empowers the people of God for the mission of God, we must not miss the image of God in everyone waiting to be activated by the imagination of God. Real church growth is energized by the greatest unique capacity we have as humans: our ability to transcend time and space in our mind's eye, our ability to dream. We can't imagine the dance hall of disciple making without the eyes of a child again.

How Shared Preferences Cause an Energy Shortage

Church leaders share a common experience: whenever people come to wherever you are, you get energized. It does not matter where you are. If your heart is in the Upper Room, you get energized by people coming toward you there. If your heart is in the Lower Room, you get energized by people joining you there.

Let me illustrate what I mean. As I said at the beginning of this book, if your heart is in the Lower Room as a church attender, your emotional attachment is to the place, personality, programs, or people of the church. These are the things you like about your church. So you get energized when you see more people come through the door and stick around, because they evidently like what you like, and that feels good. There may be sincere spiritual overtones to the feeling ("Look at all the people coming to study the Bible on Thursday morning!" if that's your preferred program), but the energy boost still comes from the experience of *shared preferences* with others.

Whenever lots of people are coming to worship and participating in programs, the whole church can feel very energized—it's heady stuff. But no matter how much energy Lower Room popularity generates, it's never enough to motivate genuine disciple making. Shared preferences do not charge a person up to grow as a disciple; they certainly do not motivate someone to *make* a disciple. Shared preferences once provided enough energy to grow or at least sustain the church as an organization, but increasingly they do not supply enough even for that, judging by weekly attendance.

Shared preferences do not provide enough energy for disciple making because they do not touch the wellspring of change in a person's life, the imagination—especially the story the imagination spins in which the person is the main character.

Everyone Lives in a Story

No one can live without a story to explain their life, the world around them, and the circumstances that befall them. It has even been said that in the face of hard-to-understand experiences, if you don't give a person a story, they will make up their own. In other words, a person will use their imagination to create a picture of how things fit together, a governing metaphor or narrative that makes sense of what by itself does not make sense. Putting things in their places to show how they fit in a greater whole is what we call *meaning.*

Meaning is sort of like augmented reality—the feature in mobile apps and digital wearables that superimposes labels onto whatever picture is coming through the camera (for example, the rabbit ears on your daughter's video call or the dining hours and reviews of a restaurant hovering over its image on the screen). Meaning is the layer of labels we map onto the life we live so that it makes coherent sense.

James McClendon uses the term "tournament of narratives" for the grand metaphors that people embrace to explain their lives. Brent Curtis and John Eldredge give the following examples. Some people escape into artists' created stories—a soap opera, a comic book universe—and immerse their minds in it whenever they can. Some imagine the story of victimhood—that the world exists to oppress them, and they are helpless. Others agree that the world is hostile, but they imagine life as a battle, a merciless competition for survival. Many prefer the story of romantic love, that life is about finding the person to whom they can say, like Jerry Maguire, "You complete me." Some imagine the story of family, that eternal life arrives when their offspring thrives. Of course there is the story of success in personal achievement as the key to life. Then sports fanaticism comes from imagining that someone else's success is my own, that *we*—not only the players on the field but everyone wearing the colors—are number one.[2]

These are some of the unexamined narratives of imagination inhabited by the people who walk into your church each Sunday. They cannot distinguish these augmented realities running their lives from the objective world.

I say "running their lives" because our imaginations directly influence our motivations. Any decent story has not only characters but also a plot. The plot is driven by some problem, some conflict that the main character is trying to overcome. Another way to say it is that there is a *should* built into every story. If a person imagines life as a battle, they *should* fight for victory. If life is a romance, they *should* win or be won by their beloved. If life is a quest of discovery, they *should* ferret out the explanation of things.

A person's imagination, then, is so powerful because it tells them not only what the world around them means but also what they are supposed to do in it. So if you want to change a person's life for real, you have to win them over to a new grand metaphor in a renovated imagination.

The Trap of Lower Room Imagination

Unfortunately, the church often misses its chance to win over people's imaginations. I am not just talking about drearily visionless churches. I mean churches whose leaders try hard to inspire life change by giving people a new story, but it falls flat. I am talking about the lesser imagination of the Lower Room.

I have spent my life helping church leaders marshal effort and investment for the church's vision. I regularly teach six elements of compelling vision, including *the Golden Tomorrow* (describing the vision as the better tomorrow in which the listener will want to live) and *the Mind Stretch* (expanding the imagination with audacious, God-sized goals).[3] With principles like these, I have tried my best to help pastors master the communication moment.

Yet not even church leaders are exempt from fighting in the tournament of narratives. We too live in the augmented reality generated by our imaginations, particularly what we imagine church growth to look like. If the image of church growth that governs a leader's mind is a packed house on Sunday morning to hear the dynamic communicator, that image will shape how the leader attempts to motivate people.

At the end of the day, I have never doubted the intentions behind the *big why* when I work with church leaders on their vision. But I now wonder about the size of their inner story. I think about the governing narrative that may be subversively guiding their vision (and for that matter, my own). When it comes to casting a vision for the church, how much is about expanding the footprint, elevating the brand, or drawing in more people as ends, not as means? How much is a leader trying to rally support for the personal success story in their own imagination?

Sometimes, even though the Lower Room vision story is too small, it wins some degree of support anyway, because many people feel they ought to contribute to the church. But their commitment only goes so deep. Even if a person gives a sizable amount of money to a capital campaign, that may not indicate much; if the person has means, it is often easier to give money than to give themselves. People may temporarily assist the story behind the leader's imagination, but that is a far cry from making it their own. People know they *should* care, but if it is ultimately someone else's story and not their own, why *would* they care?

Trying and failing to win people to a Lower Room vision is frustrating. But think for a moment about the consequences of succeeding—of firing people up for the Lower Room of your church as the best thing they can imagine.

People who get comfortable in the Lower Room might not be in church because they have a God-soaked imagination. Instead, they might be finding benefits in the Lower Room that fit nicely with their small-scale imaginations. A savvy leader might have figured out how to feed people's desires for place, personality, programs, and people well enough that they keep coming back. The result is a sweet spot for both the attenders and the leader.

For instance, picture Curtis, a church attender whose biggest story in his imagination is winning the battle for more sales at work. If a church leader figures out how to invite Curtis into a program that is full of business contacts, Curtis keeps coming back. Or picture Janelle, whose highest narrative is finding the ideal husband who will rescue her from single motherhood. If a leader gets Janelle into a regular social circle where she can meet eligible, well-resourced men, Janelle keeps coming back. The leader might not even be aware that these are the reasons that Curtis and Janelle participate in church, but either way the leader is rewarded with more attenders.

In a Lower Room sweet spot, when the leader gives people what they want, which does not disturb and may even reinforce their small-scale imaginations, their attendance *reinforces the leader's own small-scale imagination.* If the largest story in the pastor's imagination is "we advance the kingdom when more people show up on Sunday," what happens? The preaching event may console, it may even instruct, but it does not reimagine a greater story, God's alternative story that people enter together, which truly changes their lives as disciples of Jesus. Instead, both pastor and people fortify each other's imaginations of the stuff of this world.

I know this may sound too strong. But think about it: even when a pastor attempts to unlock God's word and God's world in the preaching event, the reigning paradigm of church may still be imprisoning both the communicator's and the listeners' imaginations. The preaching moment is still bounded by the rules of eight ball, as it were. The pastor never consciously says, "I prefer keeping myself and my listeners in a smaller story," but everyone leaves church winning, so to speak, in their smaller stories nonetheless. The shared preferences of a great facility, an engaging music style, chemistry with the pastor's personality, and a few friends at church—not to mention whatever other benefits may accrue to an attender's personal governing story—become the basis of attendance. The meaning is limited to the Lower Room. So why would a pastor risk the disruption of a larger story? A smaller story may be better at winning immediate attention and attendance—everything seems to be going just fine.

The Strong Incentives for Weak Imagination

No pastor would lock their people in small stories on purpose. But pastors and people alike are stuck in an invisible system that needs imagination to stay small for it to keep going.[4]

At its best, Program Church is a we-can-do-it-you-can-help system. Senior leadership has a genuine dream for reaching the community for Christ and a strategy for doing so. That strategy needs a workforce—volunteers who staff the activities on the church's calendar and the behind-the-scenes operations that make it all go.

But what would happen if one of those volunteers got their own kingdom dream? The system is typically not designed to facilitate it. If the person wants to pursue a unique dream from God, they usually have to do it outside the church system. Yet the moment the person shifts the investment of their limited time and energy toward fulfilling that dream, the church may lose the person's volunteer hours.

Consequently, in Program Church, leaders are rewarded when people suppress their personal calling and imagination-on-mission in favor of the church's program dream. In short, there are system-wide incentives to keep people's imaginations as small as possible.

Whether in Program Church or in Future Church, vision is the outworking of all the laws that come before. When a church has a culture centered on worship services (Law 1), is powered by relevance to consumer tastes (Law 2), is validated by participation numbers (Law 3), imports attenders out of their contexts (Law 4), runs on managing programs (Law 5), and is led by celebrity (Law 6), it *must* lack imagination. It *must* get its energy from shared preferences. A vision with truly shared missional imagination—shared by everyone with everyone, not a one-way fiat from the top to the rest—would blow the whole thing up in the best possible sense. Imagine it! If the Lord were to pour out his Spirit on all flesh so that young men saw visions and old men dreamed dreams (Acts 2:17), Program Church would not survive the experience.

By contrast, when a church has a culture centered on mission, is powered by the gospel, is validated by radical unity in love, is embedded in a diversity of local contexts, runs on growing people, and is led by calling, it must operate on shared imagination. There is no other way. The laws of the Upper Room themselves require an imagination stretched as wide as the heavens above—no one can walk according to the laws without being captured by what cannot be seen with earthly eyes.

The Three Primary Colors of Kingdom Imagination

Let's return again to what the Law of Vision says: *real church growth is energized by shared imagination, not shared preference*. It's the difference between feeling energized by church and *being* energized to make disciples. It is like the difference between combustion and nuclear fission. Shared preference brings the energy of burning one gram of coal. Shared imagination is like splitting the atoms in one gram of uranium-235, which produces five million times more energy.[5]

Nevertheless, despite the glory of an Upper Room imagination, leaders often fail to depict it because they fail to grasp it themselves. The evidence for shrunken imaginations is all around. For instance, consider how generic and simplistic the average church's vision statement really is. Almost daily I encounter the ocean of threefold imperatives like "love God, love others, serve the city," and "gather, grow, go." We have no definition or shared understanding of these vague formulations. There is zero clarity and no imagination that lifts people out of Program Church.

It's no wonder. Our time horizons are threefold: we get ready to execute this Sunday (one week), we prepare sermon series (one quarter), and we have to do our annual budgeting (one year). As church leaders, we have almost no verbal artifacts as evidence that we have seriously engaged our imagination to lead the people of God. The average pastor spends more time on sermon prep in four weeks than they do on vision casting over five years.

But it doesn't have to be this way. As imagination artists, we have three primary colors on our palette that we mix to paint the grand landscape of Upper Room vision. They are *parables*, *special calling*, and *local impact*. These move our language from the generic to the specific to enchant disciples' hearts. One or two of them make a decent picture, but when you skillfully blend all three, you have every color you could ever need or want to enable people to see the world they think they know in a totally new way. All it takes is time and the will to practice.

The First Color: The Parables of Jesus as the Deep Tone of Vision

Because revelation feeds imagination, the Bible is the place to find the deep color tone that forms the base of the rest of the painting. There is no better way to get started than by reading, pondering, discussing, and preaching the parables of Jesus.

Jesus's parables are ingenious because they not only convey truth, they engage the imagination with the unimaginable. Jesus uses the stuff of the present to illuminate a vision of the future. He uses what was well-known to unveil the unknowable: "'What no eye has seen, what no ear has heard, and what no human mind has conceived'—the things God has prepared for those who love him" (1 Cor. 2:9). The parables are the kingdom's operating system of thought, the basic metaphors that run the Godward life.

Parables have a way of breaking through hardened categories to reveal truths beyond conventional wisdom. Is the kingdom of God big or small? Jesus has a parable for that (the mustard seed). Is God merciful or severe? There's a parable for that too (the unmerciful servant). Is Jesus returning quickly or after a long time? There's also a parable for that (the ten virgins). Is the kingdom inclusive or exclusive? Jesus told that parable as well (the wedding feast). In a minimum of words, the parables cut knots and resolve dilemmas by stepping outside fossilized polarities to reveal harmonized paradoxes. A church that is infused with parables also nimbly steps outside many of the A-or-B, this-or-that, pick-a-side choices pressed on us by the world. Then the church itself becomes a parable of the kingdom of God.

By teaching in parables, it is fitting that Jesus used metaphor so freely, because, in a manner of speaking, he is the ultimate metaphor. A metaphor is a verbal incarnation of an idea into concrete, tangible form; similarly, Jesus is the incarnation of the Logos—the idea of Idea itself—into flesh we could see and handle (John 1:14; 1 John 1:1). Jesus did not speak parables of the kingdom because he was groping for a way to get his message across in a foreign world. Rather, God designed the world through him to exhibit him and his kingdom when he came. In G. Campbell Morgan's profound words, "He says, 'I am the true Vine.' Now, we make a mistake if we say that Jesus borrowed the figure of the vine to teach

THE LAW OF VISION **197**

us what He is. The deeper truth is this. God planted the vine in the world and let it grow through the centuries on the pattern of the infinite Christ."[6] The parables were the plan all along.

Warren Wiersbe says that a parable starts as a picture, then it becomes a mirror, and finally it becomes a window: "First there's *sight* as we see a slice of life in the picture; then there's *insight* as we see ourselves in the mirror, and then there's *vision* as we look through the window of revelation and see the Lord."[7]

Centuries before online education, Jesus used parables to provide distance learning. A parable is a *narraphor*—a metaphor in narrative form[8]—that lodges in a disciple's mind like a slow-release drug. Jesus packed layer upon layer of truth into an incredibly small span of words, and it continued secreting a deeply vibrant vision of the kingdom into the memory of Jesus's disciples long after he left earth. The power of the metaphor kept changing people years after they first heard it.

Parables, then, are vitamins for the believer's imagination. They are the inheritance of the whole church, but they also nourish the imagination of *each* church. All believers are to have imaginations satisfied on the full buffet of the metaphors of the Lord. Yet there are certain pictures that lend special energy to each individual church that hint at the vision God has for it to serve him in its place and time.

The Second Color: Long-Term Local Impact as the Midtone of Vision

I have written about the unique vision belonging to each church more than I have written about any other topic. I wrote extensively on the subject in my book *Church Unique*, which introduced the Vision Frame master tool, and I followed it up with the Horizon Storyline master tool for vision casting in *God Dreams*. In both books I made the case for why it is so important for each church to get a clear vision from God for what it is supposed to do that ten thousand others could never do. Though I will not repeat chapters' worth of discussion here, I will say a brief word on the subject.

In short, is it possible that your church has a special assignment from God to fulfill that you have not yet named? Is it possible that God is yearning to give your church a fresh imagination of the gospel good that only you can display in your place and time?

People might not know it, and they might not be able to put it into words, but they desperately need an on-ramp to the superhighway of the epic story of God's redemptive work in the world. Yet it is very difficult for most people to grasp that story at the macro level of the globe unless they experience it in person at the micro level of a church (and then, by discerning their own special calling, at the nano level of their personal life).

For example, I recently worked with Good Shepherd Church, currently pastored by Talbot Davis. During a two-day dream retreat, the team began imagining what it would look like to pursue the radical decline of divorces in the five zip codes around their church. They ended up declaring a seven-year "beautiful marriage" vision and launching a movement of marriage mentors. The vivid description of their vision begins: "A pretty wedding lasts a day. A beautiful marriage lasts a lifetime. In seven years throughout our community, we will touch 10,000 married couples. We will help households prevent crises rather than manage them. We will redefine what culture says about marriage and reinforce what God says about it."

My book *God Dreams* describes what this kind of dream does to fuel the imagination and contribution of a disciple-making culture. Now the church has given something for disciples to sink the teeth of their imagination into. It's filet mignon for the mind rather than the cotton candy of a hollow gather-grow-go mantra or the fast food of the next sermon series. You simply don't care as much about the color of the church's carpet or your favorite preacher on the teaching team when you are fired up to pray for other married couples on your street.

That's what makes the unique vision of the local church the midtone of an Upper Room landscape: it mediates between the life of the individual and the work of God in the whole world. A picture of long-term local impact is like a booster rocket to God's cosmic vision for the universal church. The redemptive vision of what God wants to do through your church for some people in some place at some time transports people's imaginations to what God wants to do for all people in all places at all times. It captures them and energizes them as disciples in a way shared preferences never could.

The Third Color: Personal Calling as the Bright Tone of Vision

To finish the landscape of a kingdom vision that captures people's imaginations, we need a bright tone to gild the fine details— namely, the individual souls God has painstakingly crafted. People step into the Upper Room when they apprehend the special calling God has made them for in his grand plan.

We have already explored this in some detail in the previous chapter, but I want to drive home again how crucial personal calling is for the church to thrive in its collective calling. In particular, I want you to see how your own imagination about what your people are and who they can become can be either the greatest limiter or an exponential accelerator to real church growth.

Carl F. George observed, "Through my years of consulting, I have learned that the pastors who are going to make it in church growth . . . dare to dream and imagine that there is a better future out there than the one they have experienced. . . . I submit that the most important issue in empowerment is a holy imagination of what God can lead a person to become."[9]

When George wrote this, he was talking about a leader's imagination about *themselves*, what George called a "sanctified self-image." But apply the same idea to the people led by the leader. Do you have a holy imagination of what a person in your church can become as grand as your imagination of your own potential?

This question is critical because of the immense impact your imagination has on the people you lead. Few leaders get anywhere without the vision of a leader going before them.

J. Robert Clinton devoted his life to studying how leaders are formed over a lifetime. Near the conclusion of his magnum opus, *The Making of a Leader*, Clinton articulated a profound insight that he called Goodwin's Expectation Principle: "A potential leader tends to rise to the level of genuine expectancy of a leader he respects."[10]

You will never experience real church growth beyond the imagination you have for your people's contributions to the kingdom. I said "the kingdom," not "your church." I am talking about more than which volunteer slots they can fill. I am talking about them bearing fruit that lasts—thirty, sixty, a hundredfold—wherever they go. Is your imagination big enough to conceive the grandeur of their personal callings?

The Imaginative Virtue of Prudence

All people naturally get stuck in the tyrannical givenness of the immediacy of this world. We are inclined to function as if *this* is all there is even though we long for something more. Our calling as shepherds of the Lord's flock is to lift people's vision higher to see more than this earthly plane of preferences.

Yet it is impossible to help people see above the ground level when our own eyes are stuck on it too. Church leaders function in a relentless Sunday's-comin' world—a worship service to plan, programs to run, people to draw, nickels and noses to count. Once a year, leaders may pop their heads up at budget time, and there may be the occasional glance ahead when preparing a sermon series.

The Greeks and later the church spoke of a virtue called prudence. At first the word "prudence" might sound lame and boring. It sounds like "eat your vegetables" and "don't spoil your supper." It also sounds like "prude" (a coincidence; the words come from different origins). In other words, prudence sounds like the virtue of no fun.

But in reality, prudence means the wisdom to make good choices now in light of what is to come. It is lifting vision higher to recognize the consequences of today's actions and the dangers and opportunities of tomorrow. In short, prudence is all about imagination. It is about separating oneself from the stream-of-consciousness gerbil wheel of the day-to-day to see over the distant horizon with a vision that transforms the here and now.

The church needs more prudent leaders than ever before. Philosopher Charles Taylor writes of the "social imaginary," the shared understanding in a society about what is good and bad, what makes sense and what does not. Kevin Vanhoozer says we need an "ecclesial imaginary," a shared vision of the kingdom of God that sets the norms of the people of God.[11] The church needs its leaders to be ecclesial imagineers.

You have heard Proverbs 29:18: "Where there is no vision, the people perish" (KJV). That is because where there is no vision, the people *cherish* the stuff of this world, including their preferences for the church's Lower Room. But we may also say that where there *is* vision, the people *pastor the parish* of their local contexts by leading and growing people in Christ. Visionary imagination keeps all disciples moving the same way even when they are not in the same room, because they are all in the Upper Room, viewing this world through the augmented reality of the kingdom of God.

TWO FUNNELS

THE FUTURE CHURCH STRATEGY MODEL

FUNNEL IN

How the Assimilation Model Yields
Diminished Returns

As you've discovered, this is a book of binary contrasts: Program Church and Future Church. The functional Great Commission and the actual Great Commission. Faking disciples and making disciples. I repeatedly present this or that, A or B, and B is always better.

At first, part 3 appears to be more of the same. When you saw the title "Two Funnels," you probably guessed that I believe one funnel (whatever it is) is better than the other, and you would be right. Glancing at the subtitles of this chapter and the next only reinforces the hunch. But before I describe what I mean by a funnel and what makes one superior, we need to return again to the most important contrast of this book.

From beginning to end I have compared the Lower Room of place, personalities, programs, and people to the Upper Room of disciple-making vision. Nevertheless, it is crucial to remember that the Lower Room and the Upper Room form one house. That is the essence of Future Church. It isn't a one-story ranch (Program Church) or a beach house on stilts (House Church). It is a two-story house with both a Lower Room and an Upper Room, and each serves a purpose. A good Lower Room draws people in, but it requires a good Upper Room to draw people up. Without the Upper Room, the Lower Room goes nowhere, but a Lower Room that plays its part leverages the advantages of the institutional church for the kingdom.

These two rooms correspond to the two funnels I will describe in these last three chapters. While the two rooms depict two different places of motivation for the church attender, the two funnels describe two patterns of people movement (figure 4). The funnel of the Lower Room I call the assimilation funnel—it is about engagement in church activity. The Upper Room's is the multiplication funnel—it is about empowerment in mission activity. The assimilation funnel moves from many to few and the multiplication funnel from few to many. Like the Lower Room itself, the assimilation funnel can play a useful role in actualizing God's disciple-making vision, but without something more—the multiplication funnel—it is a dead end.

For this reason, it should disturb us that the assimilation funnel by itself is the predominant ministry model among church leaders. It contains the assumptions that have formed many of us even if we have never spoken of it in the terms I use here. The assimilation funnel is not essential to the church as God has defined it in Scripture, but it is deeply woven into the culture of most North American nonimmigrant churches that have experienced numerical growth at some time or another since 1980.

The Sales Funnel

Every funnel allows many particles to enter the wide end and a few to exit from the narrow end. Between the two ends, the space gets progressively narrower and the number of particles decreases. For this reason, the funnel has become the business world's standard image for moving sales prospects through a

Figure 4 – The Assimilation and Multiplication Funnels

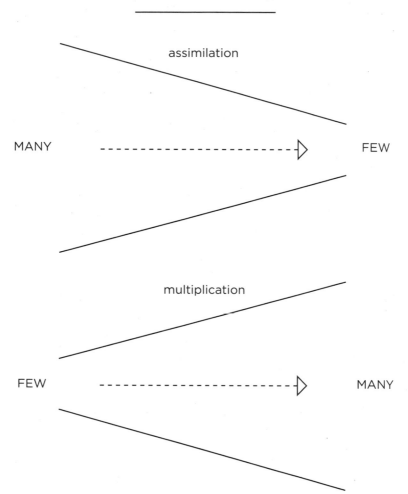

sequence of progressive steps. It maps the movement from lead to prospect to customer to referring customer—a raving fan of the product or service. The funnel shape depicts the reality that fewer people commit to each next step of engagement than committed to the step before.

For example, pretend you own an interior design firm and you want to expand to take on more clients. These potential customers are at the wide end of the funnel. You might advertise a free ebook on how to plan the perfect office redesign. Of the potential customers who learn about your ebook from online ads, search results, or digital influencers, some will give you their email address in order to download your book. Of those people, some will read your email newsletter with articles on interior design topics. Of those readers, some will sign up for the one-hour webinar you offer. Of those who attend, some will sign up for a consultation. Of them, some will sign a contract. These paying customers are at the narrow end of the sales funnel.

In this example, you started with a large number of potential clients and you ended up with a small number of actual clients. But the small outcome isn't necessarily failure. You don't need everyone in the world to contract your interior design services to grow your business. You might discover that only one of a thousand people who learn about your ebook become clients. That might be just fine—the one customer you ultimately win may more than pay for the cost of reaching the 999 who don't.

Now that you see what I mean by a funnel, transfer the model to your church. What does your church's sales funnel look like?

If your church is like most, a full picture probably looks something like the following:

- Everyone in a certain geographic area who isn't going to church is outside the funnel.
- Some of them will learn about your church.
- Some of those people will *attend* in a *worshiping environment* (i.e., a worship service).
- Some of those people will *connect* in a *relational/learning environment* (e.g., a home group).
- Some of those people will *serve* consistently in a *volunteer/ministry environment* (e.g., a ministry team).

Those who make it all the way through the funnel are qualified to become leaders, because they have been fully assimilated into the church—hence my term "assimilation funnel" (figure 5).

You may layer in other steps along the progression such as becoming a member and becoming a regular giver, but the foregoing describes the basic funnel of most church models we've become accustomed to. This progression appears everywhere in church life, for which we can thank the paradigm busters and model makers of the new permission era.

Critiquing the Assimilation Funnel

Rick Warren's *The Purpose-Driven Church* was published in 1995 and dominated church growth thinking among on-the-ground

Figure 5 – The Assimilation Funnel

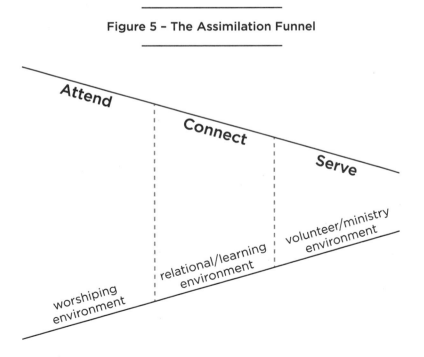

practitioners for a generation. Purpose-Driven was not the only model of the new permission era, but it was by far the best presented to the ministry-reading public, selling over a million copies. It is only a small stretch to say that church growth literature since 1995 consists of sequels to *The Purpose-Driven Church*.

One of those sequels, however, stood above the rest: Thom Rainer and Eric Geiger's *Simple Church*, published in 2006, which sold hundreds of thousands of copies. *Simple Church* represented the refinement of the new permission ministry system, distilling the model to its pure essence. For instance, what Rick Warren presented as a five-step assimilation process Rainer and Geiger reduced to the familiar three-step progression that I labeled "attend-connect-serve" above.

Books and training in the vein of new permission church growth continue to be released to this day. For instance, Church of the Highlands in Alabama promotes an increasingly popular four-step assimilation process of attend-connect-grow-serve featuring a Growth Track in which participants explore their personal gifts and how they plug into service opportunities in the church. Nevertheless, this new wave of ministry strategy is only the latest edition of the pattern set a generation ago, following in the large footprints of *Purpose-Driven* and *Simple Church* and perpetuating the model of the assimilation funnel.

> *Read how hidden contradictions in* The Purpose-Driven Church *and* Simple Church *shaped ministry for a generation at* futurechurchbook.com/bonus.

However, the eleven-year span between those two publications indicates that the new permission model was maturing just as the missional reorientation was getting underway. For the first two decades of this century, then, other voices spoke up to critique the assimilation funnel against their own understandings of disciple making.

One representative, Randy Frazee, critiqued how the funnel detached believers from their local contexts of evangelism, namely their neighborhoods. Jim Putman critiqued the funnel's absence of life-on-life, relational disciple making. Even the staff at Willow Creek Community Church, the other great progenitor of the new permission era beside Warren's Saddleback Community Church, critiqued the failure of their own process to generate life change when they measured program participation against true discipleship outputs.[1]

I respectfully join these voices to critique a Lower Room–only assimilation funnel against the Seven Laws of the Upper Room:

- **The Law of Mission.** The assimilation funnel starts with getting people into worship services, not equipping disciples for mission where they live, work, and play.
- **The Law of Power.** The assimilation funnel works when it attracts a crowd, not when it delivers the gospel through disciples to the crowd cloud surrounding them every day.
- **The Law of Love.** The measure of disciple-making success in the assimilation funnel is the flow of numbers across programs, not the supernatural unity evident among disciples.
- **The Law of Context.** The assimilation funnel is based on attraction and centralization from a wide area, not the limitless diversity of local context that can only be penetrated by dispersed disciples.
- **The Law of Development.** The programs of the assimilation funnel major on information transfer en masse, not the individualized development of reproducing disciples.
- **The Law of Leadership.** The wide end of the assimilation funnel requires the attraction of a dynamic communicator and musicians, which elevates celebrity over the diverse callings of the body of Christ to be pastors where they are.

"Assimilation" itself means making people the same, folding them into an undifferentiated mass—the opposite of empowering individuals' God-given uniqueness.

- **The Law of Vision.** When leaders' imaginations are influenced by the assimilation funnel, they are prone to get energized by people showing up at church, rather than dreaming about the dramatic gospel impact they and their church family will have in the future.

More broadly, I critique the new permission model according to my Vision Frame master tool. The Vision Frame expresses a church's answers to the five irreducible questions of organized disciple making.[2] Three of the five are:

- *What are we doing?* (the question of mission)
- *How are we doing it?* (the question of strategy)
- *When are we successful?* (the question of measures)

In the attend-connect-serve or gather-grow-go or love-God-love-others-serve-the-world model, these three irreducible questions are collapsed into one. In other words, the models define the funnel as the mission of the church, and at each step of the funnel they equate attending a new ministry environment with a new discipleship outcome in the person's life.

The impulse to combine mission, strategy, and measures is understandable because simplicity is beautiful. But this overreduction is not simple but simplistic. In practice, when these three essential elements collapse into one, strategy dominates mission and measures and swallows them up.

The mission of a church, its reason for existence, ought to be marked by singularity, not broken down into five purposes or three parts. Anytime an organization misses the opportunity to state the one thing it does, it significantly dilutes the Upper Room. Misusing a strategy statement as a mission or the mission's scorecard is like using a screwdriver as a hammer or a ruler. Answering "how?" does not answer "why?" at the same time. And it misses the biggest opportunity to motivate people, as Simon Sinek reminds us in his maxim "start with why."[3]

The way this why-to-how reduction severely limits motivational and visionary communication is illustrated by Dave Rhodes's quip, "You don't tell people that you went to Toyota for vacation." You go to a *destination* on your vacation—Rosemary Beach, Florida, or Boulder, Colorado—and that's the thing you talk about. You may have driven a Toyota to get there, but that is only the vehicle, a means to get to the vacation itself. Likewise, when the mission merely delineates the strategy—the vehicles—to get to the mission, we have squandered the opportunity to make the mission itself the main point.

When the mission is framed as sequential steps in a strategic process, it leads to absurd contradictions. For instance, it implies that we glorify God when we are at a worship service or that we grow as disciples when we are at small group, but not when we are anywhere else doing anything else. To the contrary, *everything* we do as a church ought to glorify God and make growing disciples, including when people are not at church.

Worse, if the mission is identical with a program sequence, program attendance is mission accomplishment. This is the unbiblical operational logic of the functional Great Commission: "Go into all the world and make more worship attenders, baptizing them in the name of small groups and teaching them to volunteer a few hours a month."

Similarly, when measures are equated with strategy, they stop making sense. For example, the sequential processes of new permission churches often put loving God before loving others. Loving God certainly does precede loving others logically, but does loving God really precede loving others chronologically? In other words, does a new believer ever live for a period of time genuinely loving God (because the person attends a worship service) and *not* loving others (because the person is not in a small group)? Similarly, does anyone spend time loving others (because of their small group attendance) but *not* serving the world (because they aren't volunteering in the church)?

To the contrary, the Bible repeatedly teaches that it's impossible to love God without loving others or to love them without serving them (e.g., see 1 John). The only reason they are made separate stages in the assimilation funnel is that the functions don't match the label. In this model, "loving God" means singing along with a band and listening to a talk. "Loving others" means having closer friendships that keep a person personally attached to the church even when it becomes impersonal as it grows in size. "Serving the world" mainly means laboring in the church's public activities that make it more attractive to outsiders, which feeds the funnel, and staffing the church's programs for insiders, which moves people through the funnel. When spiritual growth becomes confused with funnel activity, the funnel becomes an end unto itself.

I defined Program Church as big on organization and small on disciple making. That is because, despite the good intentions and godly language of church leaders, the assimilation funnel cannot help but shape their conception of discipleship in strictly organizational terms. In the assimilation funnel, a disciple loves God in an organized worship environment, loves others in an organized relational/learning environment, and serves people in an organized volunteer/ministry environment. The expectation of disciple making itself is laid on the organization, not on the individual. When everything disciples do is tied to an organization, would any disciples survive—much less make more disciples—if the organization were suddenly removed?

I stress again that the content of preaching, small group material, and mission and vision statements in Program Church may proclaim exactly the opposite of this; they may urge individuals to be disciples who make disciples where they are. But as I quoted Marshall McLuhan in a previous chapter, "the medium is the message"—how we do what we do has a greater impact on people than what we say while we're doing it.

Perhaps the limitations of the assimilation funnel become most evident just by examining the numbers. Across the thousands of churches that my organizations have worked with, hundreds have taken customized congregational surveys. While the whole sample of churches presents a range of percentages, we have found that typically about 50 percent of those who attend also connect. Likewise, about half of those who connect—25 percent of the whole—also serve in the church apparatus on a regular basis. Try as you might to mobilize every attender, these figures won't budge very far.

To go back to the earlier illustration, a sales funnel is fine when you're winning clients. Narrowing potential customers from the

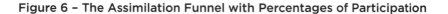

Figure 6 – The Assimilation Funnel with Percentages of Participation

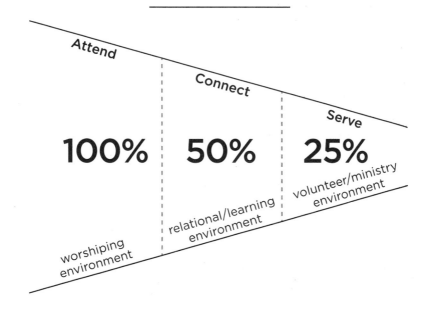

many to the few can keep you in business. And likewise, the assimilation funnel is important for engaging your folks in useful ministry environments. But if that's all you have, you'll be stuck back at the functional Great Commission. This approach in isolation will never achieve Jesus's actual Great Commission; you cannot make disciples of all nations if your model is doomed to diminishing returns. There has to be something more.

Jesus's Assimilation Funnel

Jesus knew that there was something more than the assimilation funnel. However, Jesus's own ministry proved that the assimilation funnel itself is not a bad thing, because *even he used one.*

The clue is in a well-known parable that Jesus told to the crowd but only explained to his disciples (Matt. 13:3–9). Jesus portrayed a farmer going out to plant grain by reaching his hand into a seed bag and spreading it on the ground with a backhanded toss. Some seed fell on hard earth and did not sprout. Some fell on shallow soil and did not last. Some fell on thorn-ridden ground and did not produce. Some fell on fertile soil and produced a yield thirty, sixty, or one hundred times the amount of seed the farmer spread. The end.

> ## Jesus's own ministry proved that the assimilation funnel itself is not a bad thing, because *even he used one.*

Looking carefully at Jesus's explanation of the four soils, we see that they are ordered in a specific sequence: of those who hear the gospel, some believe; of those who believe, some last; of those who last, some produce fruit. This was Jesus's assimilation funnel. It explains why he proclaimed the gospel to everyone he could, why he preached to big crowds. It was not for the reason many of us want to preach to big crowds—he did not count hearers or even believers. He counted reproducing disciples. Consequently, he spent years sifting through thousands to find dozens.

All this may make sense to us. Nevertheless, because we are not first-century farmers, we are liable to miss this parable's shocking ending. We do not immediately grasp that the crowd who heard this story must have been completely bewildered when he finished—the rabbi made no sense.

Everything about Jesus's story is a totally ordinary description of ancient agriculture until the very last sentence. The typical crop yield in Roman Palestine was only four to seven times as much seed as was planted. So the figures Jesus gave for a harvest in his story were ridiculous. Jesus's *smallest* ratio of thirty to one was *double* the crop yield of the richest soil in the entire Roman world.[4]

So what was the point of the parable? Jesus was teaching that of all the people who are exposed to the word, the few hearers who do what he says—who become fully trained as disciples—are so hugely productive for the kingdom that they far more than compensate for the many people who do not commit to being developed. This explains why Jesus spent years preaching to thousands to recruit and prepare dozens who were ready to be sent. Those few dozen would become immeasurably more than the thousands: they would explode the boundaries of Palestine and take his message across the world.

Jesus asked his disciples, "Don't you understand this parable? How then will you understand any parable?" (Mark 4:13). Grasping the paradoxical funnel of Jesus—that the narrow end far outproduces the wide end—is essential to the Upper Room imagination of the actual Great Commission.

FUNNEL OUT

How Jesus's Model Generated Multiplying Impact

W e can't adequately grasp Jesus's multiplication method—what we called his funnel in the previous chapter—until we understand how his disciple making proceeded over the course of his ministry.

For starters, we have to look again at a term frequently found in the Gospels—the word "follow." At its broadest, following Jesus meant physically going where he was to see what he was doing and hear what he was saying. There was more than one level of following, however. First, there were large crowds who followed Jesus to hear him teach and to be healed. For example, Matthew 4:25 says, "Large crowds from Galilee, the Decapolis, Jerusalem, Judea and the region across the Jordan followed him." At the same time, however, Jesus invited individuals to follow him, which meant something much more intensive—the relationship of a disciple to his teacher. Finally, Jesus authorized some of those followers to go, preach, and heal in his name, and Jesus often took these disciples to follow him without anyone else accompanying them.

In other words, Jesus interacts with three classes of followers throughout the Gospels. Many people are *listening*. These are generally known as "the crowd(s)" or "the multitude(s)." A smaller subset is *learning*. These are usually known as "the disciples," although there are some (especially women) who plainly act as disciples without being labeled as such. A still smaller subset is *going*. Sometimes they are simply called "disciples" as well, but they are often known by other titles, such as "the Twelve." Throughout the Gospels, then, Jesus is doing three things simultaneously: (1) attracting crowds who listen, (2) calling disciples who learn, and (3) sending the Twelve and others who go.

He does all three activities (especially the first two) more or less continually, yet he also exercises restraint in all three. He does not call everyone he attracts, and he does not send everyone he calls. He even tries to limit how many he attracts, vainly demanding that people he heals not spread the word. Even so, he never turns away those who insist on listening (such as the crowd that chases him around the lake in Mark 6:32–37), learning (such as Mary, Martha's sister, in Luke 10:38–42), and even going in his name without explicit authorization (such as the anonymous exorcist in Mark 9:38–40), even when other followers want him to stop them.

The second preliminary to understand is the timeframe of Jesus's ministry, which students of the Gospels have tried for centuries to piece together by comparing Matthew, Mark, Luke, and John. Estimates of the total length of Jesus's ministry have ranged from several months to almost four years. One possibility is that Jesus operated over a two-year period. He was baptized not long before a Passover celebration (John 1:29, 43; 2:1, 12–13). A major transition occurred in Jesus's ministry around the next Passover (John 6:4). And Jesus was crucified and raised from the dead at the Passover after that.[1]

Looking at Jesus's ministry this way, we see a pattern emerge of how he made disciples and prepared to multiply. The pattern repeats itself each of Jesus's two years of ministry:

- Jesus starts with no followers or drastically reduces his followers.

- Jesus attracts listeners and calls learners.
- Jesus sends goers.

This pattern is the essential backdrop of Jesus's multiplication funnel.

Jesus's First Year

To understand how Jesus launched his disciple-making ministry, we first must confront the Gospels' differing accounts of what happened in the days following Jesus's baptism. The Synoptic Gospels (Matthew, Mark, and Luke) state that Jesus went into the wilderness to be tempted by the devil; characteristically, Mark says this happened "immediately" (1:12 ESV). By contrast, John describes weeks or months of activity with an early group of disciples that began literally the day after Jesus's baptism. These different accounts are difficult to reconcile. What adds to the difficulty is that it is unclear how much each Gospel is arranged thematically instead of chronologically.[2]

One way to reconstruct the story is that the first five chapters of John describe roughly the first four months of Jesus's ministry, and the chapters of the Synoptics that depict Jesus's early ministry describe the following period of about eight months. But even if this chronology is not quite right, debating the details does not nullify the big pattern that any reader of any of the Gospels can see: Jesus rapidly attracted crowds of listeners and called a smaller number of learners (disciples), and at critical moments he sent some of the learners on mission as goers.

Jesus Starts with No Followers and Attracts Listeners and Calls Learners

From day one, Jesus begins attracting a crowd and calling disciples, although at first it is John the Baptist who does it for him.

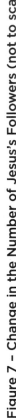

Figure 7 – Change in the Number of Jesus's Followers (not to scale)

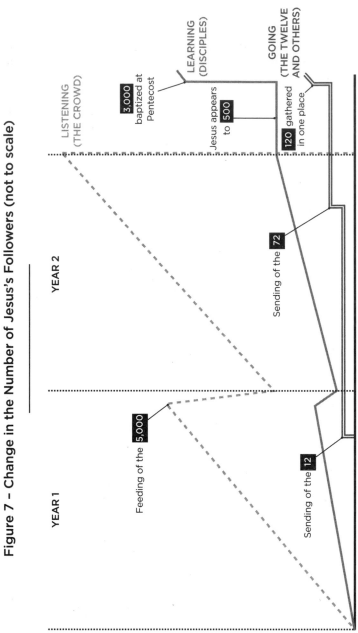

YEAR 1   YEAR 2

LISTENING
(THE CROWD)

LEARNING
(DISCIPLES)

GOING
(THE TWELVE
AND OTHERS)

3,000 baptized at Pentecost

Jesus appears to 500

120 gathered in one place

Feeding of the 5,000

Sending of the 72

Sending of the 12

Huge crowds—mostly Judeans from southern Palestine—are listening to John and being baptized by him (Matt. 3:5; Luke 3:7). John draws their attention to Jesus by calling him "the Lamb of God, who takes away the sin of the world" (John 1:29). The next day John makes the same demonstrative remark to two of his disciples, who take the hint and start following Jesus (John 1:35–37). Over a day or two Jesus acquires a group of disciples that he takes with him to his native region of Galilee in northern Palestine. A short time later, Jesus takes them on a trip to Jerusalem for the Passover and garners a lot of attention there and in Samaria on the way home (John 2:13–4:42).

Once Jesus establishes himself in Galilee, however, his popularity explodes. Awed by his power to heal, crowds are attracted to Jesus from every direction (Matt. 4:24–25), but Jesus is never content merely to attract a crowd. Instead, he makes a major effort to call disciples. This time it is not for a short-term tour or part-time study, however; now he requires disciples to leave their jobs and follow him everywhere, which Peter's calling dramatically displays (Luke 5:1–11). Yet this is not too high a bar for recruitment, because after some months, Jesus has enough disciples that Luke can call them a "large crowd" (6:17).

Jesus Sends Goers

Around this time, Jesus makes his first move to organize a third level of followers. These are the apostles—envoys who are sent with the authority of the sender. Out of his large pool of disciples, Jesus selects twelve, "that they might be with him and that he might send them out to preach and to have authority to drive out demons" (Mark 3:14–15). The apostles have a different status than the rest of the disciples and also a different task; although they are continuing to learn (with considerable difficulty), they are also authorized to preach.

At first the Twelve do not do anything different from the rest of the disciples. (When we see the words "the disciples" in these early chapters of the Synoptics, we should picture a larger group than the Twelve.)[3] But eventually Jesus sends them in pairs to do the job he chose them for: proclaiming the coming kingdom and healing people throughout the Jewish communities of Lower Galilee. At this point, multiplication officially begins; there are now in effect multiple Jesuses moving through Galilee, which thoroughly disturbs the area's ruler, Tetrarch Herod Antipas (Luke 9:1–9). Yet this dramatic expansion of Jesus's disciple-making ministry also sets up a jarring turning point at the transition from Year 1 to Year 2.

Jesus's Second Year

Jesus Drastically Reduces Followers

The turning point comes at the run-up to Passover (John 6:4). After the Twelve return from their mission practicum, Jesus takes his disciples out of the area by voyaging a little more than two miles along the shoreline to the area near Bethsaida, out of Antipas's territory (Luke 9:10).[4] Jesus and his disciples take a single boat, which strongly suggests that for the first time Jesus takes only the Twelve away with him and leaves the rest of his disciples behind—a pattern repeated through Jesus's second year.

Yet on a trip that short that nearly hugs the shore, Jesus cannot stop the rest of his disciples from following him by land along with an enormous crowd of five thousand men and their families. Out of compassion for the crowd, Jesus teaches them and then miraculously feeds them. In these respects, Jesus remains welcoming. But when he returns to Galilee the next day, he takes decisive action to reduce his following by insisting that those who want an association with him have to eat his flesh and drink his blood. This drives many disciples away and presumably turns off some of the crowd as well, although other disciples, including the Twelve, stick by him (John 6:59–69). Jesus seems to be unconcerned, because his goers represent the future of his disciple-making movement.

Jesus Attracts Listeners and Calls Learners

Nevertheless, throughout Jesus's second year, his popularity grows once more. Crowds seem to surround him at every opportunity. New learners appear to join the larger group of disciples or at least attempt to do so (Luke 9:57-62).[5]

Over the year, Jesus returns south to the Jerusalem area for ministry at least three times. On the first two journeys—the Feasts of Tabernacles (John 7:1-10:21) and Dedication (Hanukkah, John 10:22-42)—he barely escapes with his life. On the third, raising Lazarus from the dead sends Jesus's popularity soaring so high that the Sadducees on the Council finally agree with the Pharisees that Jesus must be eliminated the next time he comes to Jerusalem, even though a silent minority of leaders actually believe him (John 11:1-54; 12:42-43).

Jesus Sends Goers

Nevertheless, "when the days drew near for him to be taken up, he [Jesus] set his face to go to Jerusalem" one last time—the third and final Passover of his ministry (Luke 9:51 ESV). This will be the decisive moment that Jesus completes his mission.

But a few months before Jesus sets out, he also prepares the way by promoting more learners to goers—a lot more. Jesus appoints "seventy-two others"[6] (that is, other than the Twelve) to go in pairs to preach the kingdom and heal in every location on the way from Galilee to Jerusalem (Luke 10:1). Jesus's appointment of the seventy-two indicates that even though he has devoted increased attention to the Twelve during his second year, he has not neglected training the rest of his disciples. By the run-up to the Passover, Jesus has multiplied his missionaries by a factor of seven to a total of eighty-four.

The number of Jesus's listeners has also risen to a new peak. When he finally enters Jerusalem, it is with enough disciples to be considered a "multitude" (Luke 19:37 ESV), not to mention the crowds of Galilean pilgrims and fascinated Judeans (John 12:17–19).

The Church's First Months

The birth date of the church is generally considered to fall on the Pentecost after Jesus's ascension, but from the perspective of Jesus's disciple-making pattern, the launch of the church begins with his trials and death. All three elements of the pattern appear in the two months between Passover and Pentecost but in a different order.

First, as at the prior Passover, *Jesus drastically reduces his followers*. This time he does not lose any disciples except Judas Iscariot, "the one doomed to destruction so that Scripture would be fulfilled" (John 17:12). He does, however, lose his entire crowd of listeners when he dies. Yet it is worth noting how many learners remain after his death. At one point after his resurrection he appears to five hundred people, which we may reasonably surmise includes all of his disciples at that point (1 Cor. 15:6).

Second, *Jesus sends goers*, once again increasing their total number. Those who run into the streets to preach the gospel in other languages at Pentecost may be estimated at 120, the size of the group that formally replaced Judas Iscariot with Matthias (Acts 1:15–26). To review, near the end of Jesus's first year of ministry he had twelve he was willing to send out on mission. One year later he increased that number by a factor of seven (12 + 72 = 84). A few months later he increased the original number by a factor of ten (figure 8).

Third, this is the first time that Jesus increases the number of goers ahead of attracting listeners and calling learners. With the power of the Holy Spirit on the 120, the results are dramatic: in one day the number of listeners goes from zero to tens of thousands and the number of learners goes from five hundred to thirty-five hundred (Acts 2:41).

Figure 8 – Jesus's Multiplication Funnel of Goers

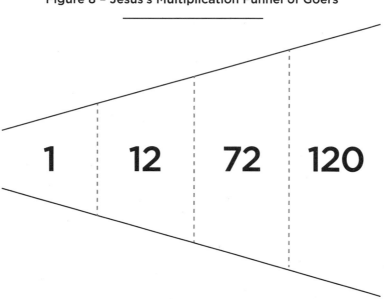

Lessons from Jesus's Disciple-Making Pattern

We took this tour of Jesus's disciple-making ministry to glean insights for how we can do the same. Jesus displays a multiplication funnel with very different results from the diminishing returns of the assimilation funnel. Yet Jesus's example also suggests that the multiplication funnel does not contradict attractional ministry—in fact, when the priority is in the right place, the two go hand in hand.

The following are three lessons from Jesus's disciple making for us to ponder.

First, Jesus was highly attractional but built nothing on the listeners he attracted. It is true that Jesus tried to modulate how much attention he got so that he would not be killed before his time. Yet he accepted John the Baptist's promotion of him, and he made his first big splash by driving merchants out of the temple on the busiest day of the year. He traveled from village to village, and he healed every sick, disabled, and demonized person brought to him. He scattered the seed of the message of the kingdom as broadly as he could within Israel. There were thousands upon thousands of people around him as often as they could get near him.

Jesus was highly attractional but built nothing on the listeners he attracted.

Paradoxically, however, Jesus placed none of the weight of his ministry on the crowd. He did not make money from it and he did not build any physical or human structure for it. He held the crowd so loosely that he severely cut it down twice (the second time, at his death, all the way to zero), and losing it had no impact whatsoever on his personal activity or the success of his ministry.

To put what Jesus did in terms I have used in this book, Jesus's church was not House Church. It was Future Church with a robust Lower Room—in fact, the best imaginable, thanks to the power of the Holy Spirit to heal people of disease and feed them bread. Nevertheless, Jesus had no resources invested in the Lower Room. He built no building, he hired no staff, and he took no salary. He and his disciples survived on the periodic generosity of wealthy women who followed him, but they did not know where their next meal was coming from.

Jesus's Upper Room did not rest on his Lower Room. It was built on pillars that drove through the Lower Room to the foundation. The Lower Room could be and was demolished, yet the Upper Room still stood. Jesus went on without missing a beat; he had nothing to lose.

Second, Jesus called learners who were highly committed and winnowed out those who weren't. He was constantly on the lookout for new disciples. He acted on the assumption that his real church was far smaller than those who got a piece of him here or there. His heart broke for the masses of wayward people, yet he seemed to embrace the reality that only a tiny fraction of them would follow him to the end and do what he said.

Jesus ensured this would be so by making discipleship not only as exciting as possible but also as risky as possible. It wasn't long before he told people to leave their jobs, not to bury their parents, and not even to say goodbye to their families. They did not know where they would sleep each night, but they did know they were associates of a wanted man. He told them to expect to be crucified. And if that was not enough, one day he appeared to demand that they become cannibals. Anyone who could tolerate all of that and still stick around was a learner indeed.

By this standard, it should be evident that in most churches, the actual number of true learners is considerably less than the number of worship attenders, even fewer than small group attenders. Indeed, many of us leaders ourselves may not qualify.

Third, Jesus invested in goers and preserved them above all else. Jesus's ideal that every disciple would become a disciple maker is implicit in his Great Commission. But it is not for nothing that he initially delivered that commission to the Eleven. He accepted the practical reality that at each moment there would be fewer goers than learners even though the numbers of both kept increasing.

Once Jesus chose disciples whom he could send in his name, they got the best of his time. He clearly chose them well: of all of them, only Judas Iscariot fell away. What qualified the Twelve for their missionary role was certainly not intelligence or insight; their thickheadedness is well known. Their main qualifications were that when he called them, they came; where he sent them, they went; and they did not give up until Jesus was arrested (as the Scriptures foretold they would). After they received the Holy Spirit, none of them gave up, even when they themselves were arrested.

Read a director's cut of this chapter that details how Jesus pastored a multisite church at futurechurchbook.com/bonus.

Jesus's disciple-making pattern and multiplication funnel are in many ways alien to Program Church. Yet the Lower Room is where modern ministry leaders find themselves and the people they serve. The art of Upper Room leadership is to take these lessons of Jesus's funnel and superimpose them on the assimilation funnel—in effect, to operate as Jesus did in the first century in the context of the institutional church of the twenty-first century. That balancing act is the essence of leadership in Future Church.

FUNNEL FUSION

How to Make Disciples without Abandoning the Institutional Presence of the Church in North America

Attention: this chapter is for one reader—the kind of leader who wants to forge a Future Church.

It is not for a leader who is content to serve Program Church, to shore up the Lower Room, and to pack people into the assimilation funnel despite diminished interest and diminishing returns. It is also not for a leader whom God is calling to give him- or herself to House Church, to advance Upper Room disciple making through a multiplying, light-footprint, low-organization expression. (If this is you, may God bless you!)

This chapter is for a leader who has caught a vision of the Upper Room and wants to live there, a leader who is on fire for its Seven Laws but is bonded to the institutional church as we know it in North America. The leader may be employed by such a church, so the bond may have financial or career threads. Deeper than that, they may be tied by memory and affection for how the institutional church profoundly impacted their own life for good.

But at the deepest level, this leader is bonded to the church by compassion. They look at the people of their church the way

Jesus looked at the throngs of the sick and weary (most of them faithful Jews, "church people"), who were "harassed and helpless, like sheep without a shepherd" (Matt. 9:36). This leader knows that deep down, their people want more, even if they cannot name it, even if they sometimes resist it. The leader does not want to abandon these people in the name of winning the lost, because in a way the people living in the Lower Room are still lost too—perhaps not lost for eternity but missing out on the glorious fullness of life God has for them in his kingdom right now.

This leader also recognizes the strategic importance of the visible church with a public profile. It remains a testimony to the world that living as a Christian is a viable option in our place and day. Done well, it can serve as evidence that Christians are a pillar of a community, because a community must have reliable institutions that give more than they take if it is to thrive. Done even better, it can be an engine of kingdom multiplication, not religious maintenance.

The leader I am talking about is called and committed to renovate Program Church into Future Church. The question is *how.*

This chapter puts it all together by combining the assimilation funnel of the new permission era with the multiplication funnel of Jesus. I want to overlap and integrate a funnel of engagement with a funnel of empowerment. This is the leadership blueprint for constructing Future Church. I do not cover much in the way of techniques or tools here; those are to come in a subsequent volume. Instead, I display a new mental model and a basic plan for leaders called to Future Church. I call it *funnel fusion.*

Upper Room leadership starts by superimposing Jesus's multiplication funnel on the new permission era's assimilation funnel (figure 9).

Funnel fusion consists of two broad steps. The first is to *build the Upper Room community*—to disciple people in the assimilation funnel so that they opt into the multiplication funnel. This is the funnel where we revive disciple-making measures. After the

Figure 9 – Fusion of Assimilation and Multiplication Funnels

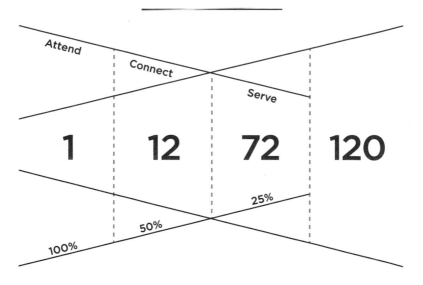

multiplication funnel is well populated, the second step is to *renovate the Lower Room*—to convert the assimilation funnel from an attend-connect-serve sequence to a listen-learn-go sequence. This is the funnel where we rehabilitate disciple-making strategy. The entire two-funnel complex is the model for renewing the church's disciple-making mission.

Step 1: Build the Upper Room Community

Funnel fusion begins when one person in the church is mentally and emotionally converted to the Upper Room (I will call this person *the one*). The one can be in any position in the church—the senior pastor, a staff member, an empowered leader, a member, even an unassimilated attender. (Obviously, I hope that the lead pastor is excited!) Holy discontent gestates growing awareness in the one, and when it gives birth, they see the business of the

kingdom in a whole new way. The one learns the Seven Laws of
the Upper Room and measures everything against them. They
become personally devoted to the mission of God and will pursue
it whether or not anyone accompanies them.

At this point, where the one focuses their attention is crucial for
whether the church moves toward Future Church. Since the one is
committed to the Upper Room, they are certain to spread the seed
of the word among the lost outside the church. But if outsiders
are the one's only focus, there will be no Future Church. Rather,
Program Church will continue obliviously while one participant
quietly nurtures a disciple-making ministry outside the walls.

But something different happens when the one looks to contribute to *anyone* God is growing, whether the person is in the church
or far from it, whether the person is hostile to God or a devoted
servant or at any stage in between. In this scenario, the one is
not only gospel-fluent outside the church but makes disciples of
believers inside the church. Lower Room churchgoers are converted by the one into Upper Room disciples. The one takes this
handful of assimilated church people along with them to engage
people who are not walking with God, much as Jesus took his early
disciples on a Passover trip to Jerusalem (John 2–4). Over time,
the one trains new believers and churched people alike in living
by the mission. They are coached to seek disciples themselves.
They eventually move on from being mere learners; they become
goers. They are *the twelve.*

The twelve—many of them anyway—are still good church
people; they attend worship and participate in a small group. But
unlike most people connected with the church who are in the assimilation funnel but not in the multiplication funnel, the twelve
now look at the church and kingdom activity differently. In particular, the twelve follow the example they were trained in by
the one, which involves training others. This gives rise to a third
generation of goers who make disciples alongside the people who
trained them. Together, these goers make up *the seventy-two.*

When a third generation of disciple makers arises, the mental model of the church begins to change. Disciple making is no longer a covert activity or the hobby of a few. A critical mass has begun prioritizing the Upper Room and living in it. Genuine, biblical disciple making begins to be thought of as a thing that *we* do, not a thing that *they* do. Leaders begin to imagine and plan what a genuine Future Church would look like, but change begins to be felt in the church ahead of any formal announcement because some of the twelve and the seventy-two begin dropping out of volunteer service. With so much fruit to harvest in the lives of people inside the church and out, they simply do not have time to maintain the ministry machine at the same level they used to.

Despite the strain on staffing programs, structural changes are still minor until a new threshold is reached—the emergence of a fourth generation of goers. More than ever before, the bulk of genuine, fruit-bearing ministry is happening outside formal church structures. *The 120* have blurred the line separating ministry inside and outside the church, because church is no longer conceived as a collection of programs and the people who staff and frequent them. The church is now seen as an interconnected web of disciples engaging the crowd cloud with gospel sharing and gospel living.

From Delivery to Disciple Making

Being the one in your church who is an empowered leader requires you to prioritize new activities and measures over old ones. For quite a while, however, no one else will notice, because you will not run new programs but take a new posture amid the programs you are already running.

One aspect of the new posture is *exploiting programs for disciple making while you use them for delivery*. To illustrate, let's return to one of the critical moments of Jesus's ministry, the feeding of five thousand men. In the eyes of virtually everyone present that day, Jesus's activity is about the crowd of listeners. He has compassion on them, he teaches them many things, and then he works a miracle to help them practically. Even though the particular miracle is new, the basic pattern is not.

Nevertheless, the Gospels give us an unusual window into what else was going on while Jesus was working with the crowd. Recall that this episode takes place just after the Twelve returned from their mission practicum. More than any time before, Jesus makes this into a prime training opportunity for the Twelve. He gives them a challenge they cannot overcome, and he has them assist him in overcoming it. This gives them exposure to his actions, priorities, and power, which they not only saw but literally *felt*.

According to Jeff Johnson, in the feeding of the five thousand Jesus was demonstrating to the Twelve the contrast between his missional mindset and their maintenance mindset:

- Missional discerns and discovers; maintenance discusses and debates.
- Missional talks and listens to the Lord; maintenance talks and listens to one another.
- Missional believes the Lord knows what to do; maintenance believes the Lord needs to be told what to do.
- Missional believes the Lord needs nothing to do something; maintenance believes there is not enough money.
- Missional believes the Lord is present; maintenance believes the location is bad.
- Missional believes there is time for the Lord to do something new; maintenance believes the day is past and it is too late.
- Missional focuses on what we have; maintenance focuses on what we lack.[1]

So who were the main beneficiaries of this ministry event? The crowd got bread, but the Twelve got experience. Jesus did not need to involve them to get the job done, and he certainly was not discussing things with them because he needed their advice. Rather, Jesus involved the Twelve because while he fed the bellies of thousands with bread, he fed the minds of the Twelve with a paradigm. As the one, Jesus was drawing a few into the Upper Room at the same time he was serving the many in the Lower Room. The food that the thousands ate satisfied them for a day; the revelation Jesus gave the Twelve lasted for a lifetime.

> Jesus fed the bellies of thousands with bread. He fed the minds of the Twelve with a paradigm.

In your own ministry, when you are feeding a crowd of listeners at Sunday morning worship or at the weekly student event, do you have a twelve that you are feeding as well? Who are you training? Funnel fusion begins when your priority in the big event is not Lower Room delivery to the many but Upper Room discipling of the few even as both are happening simultaneously.

The funnel overlap creates many avenues for the Law of Development to play out. Just as the Twelve were equipped and stretched through dynamic involvement in the process of feeding the five thousand, so your Upper Room community is equipped and stretched through dynamic involvement in program delivery.

The more imagination you exercise in applying the principle, the more opportunities emerge for Upper Room community. For instance, instead of preaching for five more minutes on the application of a main sermon point, invite an Upper Room disciple to share a real-life story. As another example, the typical church has small group or Bible study leaders who feel underappreciated filling roles in the assimilation funnel. How might an unofficial cluster of Upper Room disciples be empowered to bless, encourage, and strengthen these volunteer program leaders in the ten-minute mingle before and after a worship service?

From Platformed Programming to Ministry Practice

A second aspect of funnel fusion is *breaking the equation of ministry and programming*. In church work, if we come to the conclusion that we need to do something, our Lower Room reflex is to create, adopt, or co-opt a program for it. This program mentality is ultimately evidenced by having a program name with logo, a line item on a budget for it, and the need to promote it in worship. That is not necessarily a wrong move; it just is not the only move. Intentionality and programming are not the same thing. We can all think of programs that are not intentional about what they are supposed to accomplish. But leaders rarely think about intentional ministry practice that is not programmed on the church calendar.

My coauthor, Cory, recently led two small groups each week, both of them meeting in his home. One was advertised in the church for church people, and it counted on the church's weekly stat sheet of small group attenders. The other was an evangelistic discovery Bible study[2] of the Gospel of Mark. Both of his small groups were intentional ministry, but from a church administration standpoint, the former was a program and the latter was not, simply because it did not register as part of the system.

The very reason we have programs is to develop and equip people to practice ministry outside the programs.

Stepping into the multiplication funnel involves recognizing the existence and validity of the church's intentional ministry outside the church program. Actually, validity is not a strong enough term; in funnel fusion, the very reason we have programs is to develop and equip people to practice ministry outside the programs. If programs are not doing that, they are not doing their job.

Moving from platformed programming to ministry practice cannot be led from the rear. In other words, leaders—especially paid staff— cannot get people to do something they are not doing themselves. They cannot be so tied up with church work that they are not engaging missionally with their community in an individual, personal way. My friend Pastor Jay Cull is always saying that "you can't lead out of what you are not living into."

If church leaders are going to step into the Upper Room multiplication funnel, disciple making must be built into their job descriptions. To make it more than words on a page, enough must be taken *out* of their job descriptions to make room for disciple making in their lives.

I know of a large church whose senior pastor became so convicted about the lack of direct disciple-making activity among the staff—himself included—that each staff member was relieved of approximately 20 percent of their responsibilities, to be replaced with disciple making. For instance, the video producer had been expected to create a new video for the worship service each week. After the change, he was expected to purchase a prefab, off-the-shelf video to play one Sunday a month in order to allow him time to invest in disciples' lives. The difference in the quality of the worship experience was negligible, but the impact on the church's disciple-making culture was incalculable.

Step 2: Renovate the Lower Room

The second step of funnel fusion involves retooling and restructuring the organized church to better support disciple making. It is renovating the Lower Room to be more conducive to the priorities of the Upper Room.

Most leaders, having been shaped by the assumptions of Program Church, leap to this step immediately. They want to reshape their organization right away. Yet I stress that this is the *second* step. If you do not spend a long time converting people inside and outside the church to the Upper Room until you have generations of goers making disciples, your efforts in the Lower Room will be premature and sacrifice the missional, multiplicative momentum you began to build.

In the missional conversation there is considerable debate over whether the Lower Room *can* be renovated. The skepticism does not come only from House Church proponents either. Roy Moran describes the Future Church he has been developing in Greater Kansas City with the metaphor of a hybrid car—one vehicle, two power sources. But the substance of what he and his leaders are doing is better captured by a slightly different picture. A more apt analogy is "one operator, two vehicles," like a person driving a car and flying a drone at the same time. Moran made disciple-making goers out of people in Shoal Creek Community Church's assimilation funnel, but the newer multiplication funnel seems basically disconnected from the organized church. On the one side is an attractional new permission church and on the other is decentralized House Church. There are individuals with a foot in both, but the way Moran tells the story, they are essentially separate structures.[3]

Meanwhile, Michael Adam Beck has been pursuing Future Church in Florida from a Program Church starting point that is the complete opposite of Roy Moran's. Rather than operating from a growing, suburban, nondenominational, contemporary megachurch, Beck works with small, traditional United Methodist churches in advanced decline. In Beck's funnel fusion—which he describes with the metaphor of a blended ecosystem—there is somewhat more interplay between the deep roots of the institutional church tree and the wild branches of the shoots of light-footprint churches meeting in third spaces. Nevertheless, Beck cautions that his method of revitalization may not work in the sense of perpetuating the church organization. Indeed, he stresses that the church must be willing to die so that its gospel DNA may be birthed in new places in order for anything like revitalization to happen at all.[4]

Moran and Beck are on the leading edge of Future Church and have more hands-on experience than almost anyone you will meet, so I take their perspectives seriously. I have described Future Church as the paradigm of the next twenty years, soberly believing that it may not last beyond that. In 2040, Program Church may have disappeared and Future Church may be on its way out. In the end, Future Church may simply be a two-decades-long hand-off that allows Program Churches to be converted gradually into House Church networks.

But if Future Church would be more than a transitional zone between one structure and another—if the funnels truly would be *fused*—then the assimilation funnel of the Lower Room will have to be altered, whatever era its model came from. What then might a Future Church Lower Room look like?

Program Plus Practice

One of the great contrasts between the assimilation funnel (Lower Room) and the multiplication funnel (Upper Room) is the contrast between program and practice. The stages of the assimilation funnel revolve around which programs an attender is participating in. These programs lean heavily on information transfer, and at their best they spark insight that could change a person's life. But actually changing it requires something more—practice.

The multiplication funnel is driven by practicing the faith disciples are learning; practice is the standard of growth. Stepping into the multiplication funnel involves learning how to live as a disciple from the example of one's teacher and then passing that example on to the next disciple. As Paul wrote to the Philippians, "Whatever you have learned or received or heard from me, or seen in me—put it into practice" (Phil. 4:9).

Read a summary of what the New Testament says about practice in a disciple's life at futurechurchbook.com/bonus.

God has graciously changed the lives of many people in Program Churches. When you hear their stories, however, the change always involves practical action. For instance, a teenager meets once a week with his small group leader and follows the instructions of his mentor. A woman goes on a mission trip that requires her for the first time to serve needy people without expecting anything in return. A man receives simple tools and training for how to listen to God speak through the Bible and establishes a new habit of reading and meditating on it every day. Testimonies of life change like these always feature new steps, new habits, new practices.

Changes like this do happen in the Lower Room, but in many situations they happen almost by accident. A hundred people hear the message; one finds a way to apply it. A small group meets a hundred times; one person installs a new keystone habit from one session.

Renovating the church's Lower Room means retooling and restructuring programs to facilitate practice so that it becomes the rule, not the exception. It remodels the Lower Room in the style of the Upper Room so that the Upper Room is not so unfamiliar to people who climb the stairs.

If we relate programs to practice, we find that there are five kinds of programs.

First is *program without practice*. This is the sort of program we need to replace in Future Church. It functions solely in the assimilation funnel and at most drives people to more attendance participation but not more disciple-making process. It is the worship service that provides no more than inspiration and information, the small group that provides no more than connection and support, the ministry role that involves service without developing a new competency. You know you are leading program without practice if people can come to your church for two to three hours weekly for several years and never be engaged in modeling, practice, evaluation, and accountability around new skills for following Jesus.

Second is *program as training for practice*. This is a program that intentionally facilitates experiences for learning new skills. This is a small group not mainly on a book of the Bible but on how to study the Bible. It is a Younique cohort in gospel-centered life design that shows how to add more value to your current role at work. It is a leadership development microgroup that coaches how to navigate conflict resolution in any sphere of life.

The third kind of program is *program as practice*. As a program it belongs in the assimilation funnel, but the program's activity is all about multiplication. It is a peer-group cohort for people launching and leading discovery Bible studies. It is a prayer meeting where 90 percent of the time is spent actually praying. It is a food pantry run by the recipients of food, whose weekly distribution session involves prayer, testimony, praise, and mutual encouragement. It is a teaching team approach where emerging teachers are given opportunities to preach in worship and are coached by peers and more experienced communicators.

One common expression of program as practice is the church-has-left-the-building Sunday that came into vogue during the missional reorientation era. Instead of coming to church for one hour to hear a sermon and praise God through singing, the church attenders disperse into local service projects for the sake of their community.

Fourth is a *program to meet people for practice*. We might call this program-as-fishing-pool. This kind of program draws people into thoughtfully planned common spaces to facilitate new relationships between seasoned disciples and new or not-yet disciples. It is a book discussion that mixes opinions from a respected panel with conversation at tables. It is a seminar on finding one's way after divorce, interwoven with gospel principles, that launches an ongoing group.

In funnel fusion, every attend-and-connect environment is an opportunity for an Upper Room disciple to recruit people into unprogrammed mentoring or informal microgroups. As I illustrated earlier, in my prior role as a small group pastor, the entire purpose of our small groups was to multiply a one-to-three relational investing strategy *with people you meet inside the group.*

Fifth is *program to celebrate practice.* There are many leadership maxims about people repeating what gets rewarded. Celebration is one of the church leader's greatest opportunities not just to shape a disciple-making culture but to inspire and activate new practices by new learners and goers.

One of the favorite small groups I ever led was a neighborhood-based group of young parents (including both churched and unchurched people). We read Josh McDowell's book *How to Be a Hero to Your Kids,* which I handed out at a backyard barbecue. We really didn't need new skills as parents as much as we needed inspiration and reinforcement to live out what we already knew. As it turned out, the most substantive impact of the group time was the celebration of our minivictories as parents after a week of jump-starting better habits as moms and dads. The ten-week group was transformative almost from this element alone.

The good news is that celebration can be injected into almost any program environment, even if it is not the primary reason to create the program. Think about it: if discipleship practices were guided primarily by how you celebrate at your church, what would a disciple end up looking like?

When it comes to celebration, there is one big thing to keep in mind. Most churches celebrate what happens in the assimilation funnel, not the multiplication funnel. For example, a church celebrates when people participate in a short-term mission trip. Or they applaud the fifteen people who volunteered to build a house through a programmed event. These are good things to celebrate. But they are not the ultimate things to celebrate. The church hasn't fully engaged the Upper Room until they celebrate what happens outside of the church through the everyday practices of people. This level of reward and recognition happens when the church celebrates nonprogrammed outcomes: baking cookies for a neighbor, excelling at starting spiritual conversations, or making an integrity-based decision at work. If you watch and record what kind of service a church celebrates, nine times out of ten it is service at or through the church, not the spontaneous service of a skilled disciple.

Seven Essential Functions of Organized Disciple Making

When you consider retooling the Lower Room, it is natural to ask, "How can we make our worship, connection, and service programs facilitate practice better?" Yet that is the incremental question. The more radical question is, "If there were many disciple-making disciples in this community and no publicly visible churches, why would they create one? What would it do?"

This is a necessary question to think deeply about. We must not jump to the conclusion that these disciples would make any Lower Room at all. We have to consider soberly how much weight would already be borne by House Church that would not require replication in a large or more highly organized setting. If we do not think carefully about this, we are prone to replace one Program Church with a Program Church with different lingo and logo.

It might be impossible to extricate ourselves from our conditioning, assumptions, and rationalizations about what a Lower Room ought to look like. Fortunately, the Bible gives us a clue to the answer. Jesus, the apostles in Jerusalem, and sometimes Paul had ministries with a public profile that attracted attention. From their examples we can imagine what Future Church programs might focus on.

Here are seven functions of Future Church that benefit from or necessitate a high level of organization or visibility. They are organized in three tiers—not according to the new permission assimilation funnel of attend-connect-serve but according to Jesus's multiplication funnel of listen-learn-go.

For listeners

1. **Introducing.** Organized disciple making includes a public presence where curious people can learn what the
   Christian way is about. Jesus taught in synagogues and
   on the lakeshore; the apostles taught in the temple; Paul
   held discussions in synagogues, in Athens' agora (Acts
   17:7), and in Tyrannus's *skholé* in Ephesus, a place where
   people with time on their hands learned by dialogue
   (Acts 19:9).
2. **Healing.** Organized disciple making includes a place
   where people can be healed of what ails them. While different faith tribes today place different emphasis on
   the nature and role of healing, there is no denying that
   it was central to the public appeal of Jesus, the apostles,
   and Paul, and it formed an important validation of their
   gospel.

For learners

3. **Praying.** Organized disciple making includes mass gatherings for prayer for the mission of God and the coming of
   the kingdom. The Jerusalem church did this in the temple
   continuously as part of the ongoing worship there. Musi-
   cal prayer is an important component of this.
4. **Connecting.** Organized disciple making includes an intentional way that people who check out the Christian way
   from the fringes can enter into a deeper dialogue and even
   begin following Jesus with others.
5. **Sharing resources.** Organized disciple making includes
   a system that enables disciples to share their wealth with
   disciples in need whom they do not personally know. This
   is what the apostles and then the Seven administered, and
   Paul and others in the wider empire did likewise for the

relief of the poor in Jerusalem. Sharing also extends to honorariums for local elders (1 Tim. 5:17–18) and goers who need support on their way (as some churches supported Paul).

6. **Training.** Organized disciple making includes opportunities for kinds of training that are well suited to a less intimate, larger group setting or methodical instruction. This includes theological teaching, acquisition of certain skills (such as life design), and learning some train-the-trainer techniques. The Sermon on the Mount, which Jesus directed primarily to his disciples, may be seen as an example of this (Matt. 5:1–2).

For goers

7. **Sending.** Organized disciple making includes systems of support for goers who move outward to break new ground for the gospel as the church at Antioch did when Paul and Barnabas headed into totally unreached areas.

For most churches, it is not difficult to jam current programs into these categories and rationalize that they fit. Yet if we are honest, we usually have to admit that the way we do things today is in no way how we would do them if we were starting organized disciple making from scratch according to this blueprint.

Also take note that it might not take a heavy organizational footprint to fulfill these functions despite the church's public profile. Paid staff may be limited. Owned property may be nonexistent. Not every Future Church has to be so lean, but be prepared that a radical transformation may come from Lower Room renovation. This is why I caution that the Upper Room must be well established as the place of emotional connection for a large portion of the church before deep Lower Room work can reasonably be attempted.

The Rest of the Great Commission

Go into all the world and make more worship attenders, baptizing them in the name of small groups and teaching them to volunteer a few hours a month.

I called this the functional Great Commission of the North American church at the outset of this book. All of us know that this commission results in faking disciples instead of making disciples; at the end of the book, I hope we all know it better than ever.

But more than that, I hope we all know much better the *actual* Great Commission to "go and make disciples of all nations, baptizing them in the name of the Father and of the Son and of the Holy Spirit, and teaching them to obey everything I have commanded you" (Matt. 28:19–20).

Except that this is not the actual Great Commission.

That's right, the actual Great Commission begins, "All authority in heaven and on earth has been given to me" (Matt. 28:18). I know you know this, but have you paused to think about it recently, to roll the words around in your mind? *All authority* . . . the implications are profound beyond imagining.

Since Jesus has all authority, then of course he has the right to command us to do whatever he wants. So the Great Commission is not optional—we *must* do it.

Yet the more astounding truth is that Jesus has the authority *himself* to do whatever he wants. And that is even more astounding when we remember how the actual Great Commission ends—not with "everything I have commanded you" but with "surely I am with you always, to the very end of the age" (v. 20). The bookends of the Great Commission proclaim that this Jesus who has the right to do whatever he wants *is always with us* to do whatever he wants.

Jesus wants to go and make disciples. He wants to baptize them and teach them to do everything he commands. He wants to build his church on the rock so that the gates of death and hell will not prevail against it. He wants to seek and save the lost. He wants to give clean, white linen to his bride to wear to present her to himself spotless and blameless. He wants to redeem worshipers from every tribe, tongue, people, and nation who cry out, "Worthy is the Lamb!"

Jesus wants to do all these things. He has every right to do them. And he has never stopped doing them. Only now, he wants to share the joy by doing them with us. It is up to us to erect and perfect Future Church precisely because it is up to him.

When you go hunting for disciples who have a passion for practice, his authority and power are with you. When you reposition yourself in the church to prioritize the Upper Room over the Lower Room, his authority and power are with you. No one is in the position to tell you to stop. Jesus has all authority, and he is with you always, even to the very end of the age.

This book is an invitation to step into what you have always wanted to do, the reason you entered the Master's service. So are you ready to be *the one* where you are? Are you ready to step into Future Church?

Jesus is!

ACKNOWLEDGMENTS

We are exceedingly grateful for our dear friend Dave Rhodes, a man of great integrity, wisdom, and skill whose abiding passion is to see the church become a training center of disciples. After Will initially developed the Seven Laws, their final form evolved through long dialogue with Dave. Once Cory joined the team, a three-way collaboration continued as this book took shape. In particular, Dave helped both of us see and articulate how all the laws are connected, and his keen insight infuses many of these pages.

We are also grateful for Kelly Kannwischer, a powerful, thoughtful leader who helps us reality-check how our ideas connect to people's lives.

Many thanks go to Tessy McDaniel for her role in making our work easier and supporting Will's daily workflow.

Thanks also to James Bethany for his skill in designing the illustrations that appear in this book to our exact specifications (and his willingness to dive in at a moment's notice to help us meet a deadline!).

We are deeply grateful to our teammate, friend, and agent Don Gates for his role in securing the publishing relationship that brings this book to a wide audience. Don's experience, savvy, wisdom, and (yes) patience with us have been a great help to us all along the way.

We also express our thanks to the team at Baker Publishing Group, which has excelled in professionalism and collaboration with us every step of the way—namely Brian Thomasson, Jean Entingh, Trisha Mason, Abby Van Wormer, Janelle Wiesen, Melanie Burkhardt, Patti Brinks, Eileen Hanson, Olivia Peitsch, Erin Bartels, Rachel O'Connor, Brian Brunsting, Amy Nemecek, Rod Jantzen, Kelli Smith, Jared Kennedy, and those who started supporting us after this page went to print.

From Will

I am grateful to my wife, Romy, who graciously supports me when I take the tons of time required to put ideas on paper, giving me the love and freedom to live out my life's call. I also want to express appreciation to Romy's mother, Gladys Navarette, who has been a joyful and supportive part of our home through much of the time this book was being written. Thanks also to the rest of my central circle—my children, Jacob, Joel, Abby, and Poema.

In particular, Jacob and Joel have become new heroes to me as they passionately make disciples in their early years of full-time pastoring in the organized church. My hope in *Future Church* is made most alive in you. The words of 1 John 2:14 come to mind: "I write to you, young men, because you are strong, and the word of God abides in you, and you have overcome the evil one."

From Cory

First and foremost, I wish to acknowledge my debt to the people of the First Baptist Church of Passaic, New Jersey, and the First Baptist Church of Hollidaysburg, Pennsylvania. They taught me much wisdom (often without any of us intending it) that suffuses everything I do and say. They and their stories live in me forever.

I also wish to acknowledge Ron Short, my youth pastor when I was a teenager. I didn't know it at the time, but Pastor Ron taught me organized disciple making by discipling me (and many others) with lifelong impact. Simply put, I wouldn't be myself today without a few years of his influence at Redeemer Evangelical Covenant Church. Always ahead of his time and forever young, he practiced Future Church but not under that name. He called it "being Jesus with skin on."

Dave Bickers has been my comrade as we have seen—and sometimes *been*—the best and the worst of church. I am deeply grateful for his friendship and camaraderie as we learn disciple making together.

While *Future Church* was being written, a beautiful, ongoing dialogue with Rich Morris and Chris Weidley was unspooling new threads of insight. It is a rich joy and honor to pursue the kingdom in my calling as these brothers do in theirs. Chris and I are especially grateful for Rich's faithful leadership of Hicks United Methodist Church, where our families have found refuge.

Only God knows the make-or-break power of the prayers Ann Logue lifted up for this book's completion.

Nothing about Matt Paonessa is as big as his generous heart. Matt provided the workspace where much of this book was written and talked me off a ledge or two.

I am deeply grateful for the support of all my family, especially my parents, Daryl and Gloria Hartman.

It seems almost rude to acknowledge my wife, Kelly, as someone I could not have written this book without, because in truth, I am not sure I could have *lived* without her.

My children, Jack, Orphie, Arwen, and Israel, are acknowledged here not because they contributed to the book but because of the contributions they will make and be to Future Church itself. This project is for them.

APPENDIX

Relationship of Future Church Funnels to the Vision Frame

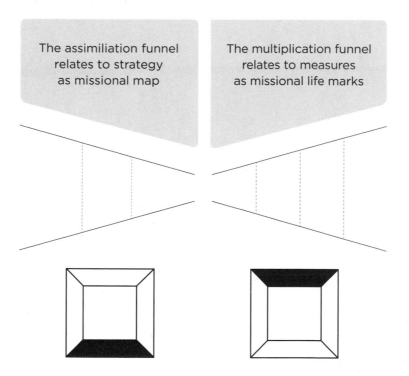

The assimiliation funnel relates to strategy as missional map

The multiplication funnel relates to measures as missional life marks

The Vision Frame master tool is described in Will Mancini's *Church Unique* and *God Dreams*. *Future Church* is a prequel to prepare a culture of real church growth before a church develops its Vision Frame.

NOTES

Chapter 1 Two Rooms: The Best Picture to Expose the North American Church's Greatest Challenge

1. Rodney Stark, *The Rise of Christianity: How the Obscure, Marginal Jesus Movement Became the Dominant Religious Force in the Western World in a Few Centuries* (Princeton, NJ: Princeton University Press, 1996), 6; Alan Hirsch, *The Forgotten Ways: Reactivating Apostolic Movements*, 2nd ed. (Grand Rapids: Brazos, 2016), 5.

2. Larry Osborne, *Sticky Church* (Grand Rapids: Zondervan, 2008), 79–81.

3. Andy Stanley, *Deep and Wide: Creating Churches Unchurched People Love to Attend* (Grand Rapids: Zondervan, 2012), 284.

4. Jim C. Collins and Jerry I. Porras, *Built to Last: Successful Habits of Visionary Companies* (New York: HarperCollins, 1994), 80–81.

5. Will Mancini, *Church Unique: How Missional Leaders Cast Vision, Capture Culture, and Create Movement* (San Francisco: Jossey-Bass, 2008); *God Dreams: 12 Vision Templates for Finding and Focusing Your Church's Future* (Nashville: B&H, 2016).

Chapter 2 Three Churches: The Most Useful Typology for the Next Twenty Years

1. Dallas Willard, "The Apprentices," on Dallas Willard's official website, accessed March 29, 2020, http://old.dwillard.org/articles/artview.asp?artID=112.

2. Ray Ortlund, Darrin Patrick, and Ryan Kelly, "How Churches Fake God's Work," *The Gospel Coalition* (blog), August 2, 2012, video file, 2:42, https://www.thegospelcoalition.org/video/how-churches-fake-gods-work.

3. George W. Bullard Jr., *Pursuing the Full Kingdom Potential of Your Congregation* (St. Louis: Chalice Press, 2005), 76–78.

4. Neil Cole, *Organic Church: Growing Faith Where Life Happens* (San Francisco: Jossey-Bass, 2005); Tony and Felicity Dale, *Simply Church* (Austin, TX: Karis, 2002).

5. Frank Viola, "House Church vs. Organic Expression," *Beyond Evangelical* (blog), October 12, 2010, https://frankviola.org/2010/10/12/house-church-vs -organic-church.

6. "How Many People Really Attend a House Church? Barna Study Finds It Depends on the Definition," The Barna Group, August 31, 2009, https://www.barna .com/research/how-many-people-really-attend-a-house-church-barna-study-finds -it-depends-on-the-definition.

7. Dallas Willard, *The Divine Conspiracy: Rediscovering Our Hidden Life in God* (New York: HarperCollins, 1997), chap. 8, NOOK.

8. Brian Sanders, *Underground Church: A Living Example of the Church in Its Most Potent Form* (Grand Rapids: Zondervan, 2018), 19–21.

9. Alvin Toffler, *Future Shock* (New York: Bantam Books, 1970), 414.

Chapter 3 Off Mission: What Keeps Leaders Serving a Functional Mission That's Not the Great Commission

1. Will Mancini, *Innovating Discipleship: Four Paths to Real Discipleship Results*, Church Unique Intentional Leader Series (n.p.: self-pub., 2013), 13–26. In *Innovating Discipleship*, I also discuss a third kind of results called *impact results*, which capture the broader effect of the church in the surrounding city or community.

2. John S. Dickerson, *The Great Evangelical Recession: 6 Factors That Will Crash the American Church—and How to Prepare* (Grand Rapids: Baker Books, 2013), 188–89.

Chapter 4 Sixty Years: How Twentieth-Century Church Growth Influences Twenty-First-Century Leaders

1. Fundamentalists of the early twentieth century were named after a series of pamphlets entitled *The Fundamentals*, which were a defense of orthodox tenets of faith against theological modernism. Although self-described fundamentalists today, one century later, trace their descent from these believers, most of their heirs began taking on the older name "evangelical" in the wartime revival.

2. The most eminent examples were the National Association of Evangelicals to replace the National Council of Churches, Fuller Theological Seminary to replace denominational seminaries like Princeton, and *Christianity Today* magazine to replace *The Christian Century*.

3. Patrick Henry, "'And I Don't Care What It Is': The Tradition-History of a Civil Religion Proof-Text," *Journal of the American Academy of Religion* 49, no. 1 (1981): 41, www.jstor.org/stable/1462992.

4. Brian Sanders, *Underground Church: A Living Example of the Church in Its Most Potent Form* (Grand Rapids: Zondervan, 2018), 15–16.

5. Rick Warren, *The Purpose-Driven Church: Growth without Compromising Your Message and Mission* (Grand Rapids: Zondervan, 1995), NOOK.

6. Warren, *Purpose-Driven Church*, chap. 12.

7. Bill Hybels, *Just Walk across the Room: Simple Steps Pointing People to Faith* (Grand Rapids: Zondervan, 2006).

Chapter 5 Attendance Uppers: Three Pills Prescribed by Church Pharma

1. Thom S. Rainer, "The Number One Reason for the Decline in Church Attendance and Five Ways to Address It," *Church Answers* (blog), August 19, 2013, https://thomrainer.com/2013/08/the-number-one-reason-for-the-decline-in-church-attendance-and-five-ways-to-address-it/.

2. Will Mancini, "Attending Church Less Frequently: The Most Important Trend of Church Trends and What to Do about It," *Will Mancini | Clarity Changes Everything* (blog), January 1, 2015, https://www.willmancini.com/blog/the-most-important-trend-of-church-trends-in-2015-and-what-to-do-about-it.

3. Carey Nieuwhof, "Why People Are Attending Church Less Often and How to Respond—an Interview with Will Mancini," *The Carey Nieuwhof Leadership Podcast*, episode 23, February 17, 2015, https://careynieuwhof.com/episode23; Carey Nieuwhof, *Lasting Impact: 7 Powerful Conversations That Will Help Your Church Grow* (Cumming, GA: The reThink Group, 2015), chap. 2.

4. Carey Nieuwhof, "5 Reasons Why Engagement Is the New Attendance," *Carey Nieuwhof* (blog), accessed September 11, 2019, https://careynieuwhof.com/5-reasons-why-engagement-is-the-new-church-attendance.

5. It seems easy to define what a multisite church is until it is attempted; then one finds that it is hard to include all the churches one thinks should be included under the umbrella and to exclude all the ones that should not. For example, it would be interesting to poll Catholic theologians as to whether they believe contemporary definitions of multisite church accurately describe the entire Roman Catholic Church or at least individual dioceses. Yet those entities are generally not what people mean when they use the term "multisite church."

6. Rez Gopez-Sindac, "Larry Osborne: The CE Interview," *Church Executive*, September 2005, 16, http://www.churchadminpro.com/Articles/Video%20Veues%20-%20Larry%20Osborne%20explains%20why%20Video%20Venues.pdf.

7. Warren Bird, "Big News—Multisite Churches Now Number More than 5,000," *Leadership Network* (blog), January 9, 2019, https://leadnet.org/big-news-multisite-churches-more-than-5000. When this site was accessed, it bore a date of January 9, 2019, but the chart in the article stops at 2012, and the article was cited by others before 2019. The article proclaiming 8,000 multisite churches in 2014 is no longer accessible on Leadership Network's website, but it is cited in Ed Stetzer, "Multisite Churches Are Here, and Here, and Here to Stay," *The Exchange with Ed Stetzer* (blog), February 24, 2014, https://www.christianitytoday.com/edstetzer/2014/february/multisite-churches-are-here-to-stay.html.

8. Jim Tomberlin, "16 Ways Multisite Churches Fail," *Outreach*, April 23, 2019, https://outreachmagazine.com/features/megachurch/42206-16-ways-multisite-churches-fail.html.

Interlude The Missional Reorientation

1. Alan Hirsch and Tim Catchim, *The Permanent Revolution: Apostolic Imagination and Practice for the 21st Century Church*, with contributions by Mike Breen (San Francisco: Jossey-Bass, 2012), 148.

2. Brian Sanders, *Underground Church: A Living Example of the Church in Its Most Potent Form* (Grand Rapids: Zondervan, 2018), 15–16.

Chapter 6 The Law of Mission: Real Church Growth Starts with a Culture of Mission, Not Worship

1. "Shorter Catechism of the Assembly of Divines: The 1647 Westminster Catechism and Subordinate Documents," A Puritan's Mind, accessed April 14, 2020, https://www.apuritansmind.com/westminster-standards/shorter-catechism.

2. Will Mancini, *Innovating Discipleship: Four Paths to Real Discipleship Results* (n.p.: self-pub., 2013), 7–9.

3. From a Protestant perspective, "the law of prayer is the law of belief" (*lex orandi, lex credendi*) gets mixed reviews. On the one hand, the principle helped the church eventually unite around the belief that Jesus is fully God, because believers had long been in the habit of praying to him as if he was. On the other hand, it later gave rise to Catholic doctrine about Mary, because people had gotten into the habit of praying to her too. My point in mentioning it is not to endorse a doctrinal principle but to affirm an *observation* of how things tend to go in the church.

4. Misha Sivan, "What Is the Meaning of 'The Medium Is the Message' by Marshall McLuhan?" *Quora* (message board), February 15, 2017, https://www.quora.com/What-is-the-meaning-of-The-Medium-is-the-Message-by-Marshall-McLuhan.

5. Dietrich Bonhoeffer, *Life Together*, trans. John W. Doberstein (San Francisco: Harper, 1954), 26–29.

6. "Special Episode: An Interview with Robert Coleman," *The Disciple Maker's Podcast*, April 19, 2018, MP3 audio file, 33:55, https://mcdn.podbean.com/mf/download/na7gw4/05-Robert-Coleman-Special.mp3.

Chapter 7 The Law of Power: Real Church Growth Is Powered by the Gospel, Not Relevance

1. "Contemporvant," YouTube video, posted by Church Soundguy, accessed February 5, 2020, https://youtube/giM04ESUiGw.

2. Walter J. Chantry, *Today's Gospel: Authentic or Synthetic?* (Carlisle, PA: Banner of Truth, 1970); J. I. Packer, *Evangelism and the Sovereignty of God* (Downers Grove, IL: InterVarsity, 1961).

3. Craig Groeschel, "Jesus and We: Anything Short of Sin," *Talk It Over* (blog), accessed March 2, 2020, https://www.life.church/talkitover/jesus-and-we-4.

4. Christopher Benek, "Afterword," in Mark DeYmaz with Harry Li, *The Coming Revolution in Church Economics: Why Tithes and Offerings Are No Longer Enough, and What You Can Do about It* (Grand Rapids: Baker Books, 2019), 238.

5. With the author's permission, this section is adapted from Cory Hartman, *From "Show Up" to "Grow Up": How to Make Top Content That Makes Real Disciples* (n.p.: self-pub., 2019), 27–28.

6. Bruce Riley Ashford and David P. Nelson, "The Story of Mission: The Grand Biblical Narrative," in *Theology and Practice of Mission: God, the Church, and the Nations*, ed. Bruce Riley Ashford (Nashville: B&H, 2011), 6–7. Ashford and Nelson use the label "biblical narrative" rather than "gospel" for these four movements, but others have explicitly used it as a gospel framework in the years since. Ashford and Nelson also use the term "restoration" for the fourth movement. We prefer "new creation," mainly because an uninformed person exposed to the model might not realize that the completed new creation

does not merely restore the creation to what it was before the fall but makes it better than ever.

7. Bill Hull and Ben Sobels, *The Discipleship Gospel: What Jesus Preached—We Must Follow*, primer (n.p.: self-pub., 2017), conclusion, epub.

Chapter 8 The Law of Love: Real Church Growth Is Validated by Unity, Not Numbers

1. Carey Nieuwhof, "Drew Powell and Matt Warren on Why Attractional Church Is Past Peak, Why It's Changing and What's Next for Weekend Services," *The Carey Nieuwhof Leadership Podcast*, episode 251, March 14, 2019, MP3 audio file, 15:55, 21:31, 32:18, 1:13:57, https://careynieuwhof.com/episode251.

2. Cory Hartman, "The Glory Spiral of John 17," *Cory Hartman* (blog), June 12, 2017, https://www.coryhartman.com/post/2017/06/12/glory-spiral-of-john-17.

Chapter 9 The Law of Context: Real Church Growth Is Local, Not Imported

1. Gilbert Bilezikian, *Community 101: Reclaiming the Local Church as a Community of Oneness* (Grand Rapids: Zondervan, 1997).

2. Originally published in 2001. The current edition is Randy Frazee, *The Connecting Church 2.0: Beyond Small Groups to Authentic Community* (Grand Rapids: Zondervan, 2013).

3. Lyle Schaller, *The Interventionist* (Nashville: Abingdon, 1997), 14–15.

4. "Architectural theorist Christopher Alexander recommends neighborhoods be defined as 'not more than 300 yards across with no more than 400–500 inhabitants.'" Frazee, *Connecting Church 2.0*, chap. 12, NOOK. With the US average of 2.6 persons per household, maximum neighborhood size comes to 192 households. ArcGIS, "2019 USA Average Household Size," https://www.arcgis.com/home/item.html?id=b597302950234000b7ba4fa33cd785eb.

5. "Our Values," Oak Hills Church website, accessed June 6, 2019, https://rock.oakhillschurch.com/page/552.

6. "Harvest Vision," Oak Hills Church website, accessed June 6, 2019, https://rock.oakhillschurch.com/harvest.

7. Bryan Rose, "Doug Paul—East End Fellowship, Richmond VA," *My Ministry Breakthrough* (podcast), episode 15, January 28, 2019, MP3 audio file, 3:26, http://www.myministrybreakthrough.com/archives/122.

8. I credit this insight to Dave Rhodes.

9. Frazee, *Connecting Church 2.0*, chap. 16.

10. C. Christopher Smith and John Pattison, *Slow Church: Cultivating Community in the Patient Way of Jesus* (Downers Grove, IL: InterVarsity, 2014), 42–43.

11. Steve Addison, *What Jesus Started: Joining the Movement, Changing the World* (Downers Grove, IL: InterVarsity, 2012), chap. 14, NOOK.

12. Erin Duffin, "Average Number of People per Household in the United States from 1960 to 2018," Statista, November 28, 2019, https://www.statista.com/statistics/183648/average-size-of-households-in-the-us.

13. For an incisive commentary on the breakdown of the *oikos*, see David Brooks, "The Nuclear Family Was a Mistake," *The Atlantic*, March 2020, https://

www.theatlantic.com/magazine/archive/2020/03/the-nuclear-family-was-a
-mistake/605536.

Chapter 10 The Law of Development: Real Church Growth Is about Growing People, Not Managing Programs

1. Robert E. Coleman, *The Master Plan of Evangelism* (1963; repr., Grand Rapids: Revell, 1993), 27.

2. Ray Ortlund, Darrin Patrick, and Ryan Kelly, "How Churches Fake God's Work," The Gospel Coalition, August 2, 2012, video file, 0:44, https://www.the gospelcoalition.org/video/how-churches-fake-gods-work.

3. Willard, *Divine Conspiracy*, chap. 8, NOOK.

4. I received this story from Dave Rhodes.

5. This section is adapted from Cory Hartman, "4 Kinds of Discipleship Content and How to Deliver Them," *Cory Hartman* (blog), https://www.coryhartman .com/post/2017/09/26/4-kinds-of-discipleship-content-and-how-to-deliver-them.

6. Some of Mac Lake's best leadership development content is a series of training guides called Discipling Leaders. The first in the series to be released is *Leading Leaders: Developing the Character and Competency to Lead Leaders* (n.p.: self-pub., 2019).

7. C. S. Lewis, *Mere Christianity* (New York: Harper One, 2015), 199.

Chapter 11 The Law of Leadership: Real Church Growth Is Led by Calling, Not Celebrity

1. The threefold temptation in Luke 4 is paralleled by the temptation of Eve in Genesis 3:1–6 ("the fruit of the tree was good for food and pleasing to the eye, and also desirable for gaining wisdom") and "everything in the world" in 1 John 2:15–17 ("the lust of the flesh, the lust of the eyes, and the pride of life"). Similarly, in Philippians 3:19 Paul spoke of "enemies of the cross of Christ" whose "destiny [or goal] is destruction" (ambition), "their god is their stomach" (appetite), "and their glory is in their shame" (approval). The LifeDrifts tool analyzes the sin beneath our sins—our persistent spiritual weakness—and how Christ overcame it on the cross on our behalf.

2. The triad of appetite, ambition, and approval are found in Mike Breen, *Building a Discipling Culture*, 3rd ed. (3DM Publishing, 2016), chap. 4, Kindle. Breen's application of the triad to American church culture (not in print) is recounted here by permission.

3. The technical term is *inclusio*.

4. Kudzu's power to smother plant life is described in Michael Graham Richard, "This Invasive Plant Is Swallowing the U.S. at the Rate of 50,000 Baseball Fields per Year," Treehugger, July 18, 2014, https://www.treehugger.com/natural-sciences /invasive-plant-swallowing-us-rate-50000-baseball-fields-year.html. A much more sober assessment of the extent of kudzu's spread (but not disagreeing with its destructiveness where it does exist) is in Bill Finch, "The True Story of Kudzu, the Vine That Never Truly Ate the South," *Smithsonian*, September 2015, https://www.smith sonianmag.com/science-nature/true-story-kudzu-vine-ate-south-180956325.

5. The free ebook is available at https://willmancini.com/clarityspiral. *Clarity Spiral* is also available in print and in Kindle format from Amazon.

6. Online Etymology Dictionary, s.v. "cleric," https://www.etymonline.com /word/cleric; *Thayer's Greek-English Lexicon*, s.v. "Strong's NT 2819" and "Strong's NT 4345." In Acts 1:17 (ESV), Peter says that Judas Iscariot had been "allotted his share in this ministry," which then needed to be reassigned to another. Peter later counseled elders to "shepherd the flock of God among you, exercising oversight . . . [not] lording it over those allotted to your charge" (1 Pet. 5:2–3 NASB). In Thessalonica "some of them were persuaded and joined Paul and Silas" (Acts 17:4 ESV); if rendered literally, the word "joined" would be "were allotted to."

Chapter 12 The Law of Vision: Real Church Growth Is Energized by Shared Imagination, Not Shared Preference

1. Alan Hirsch and Tim Catchim, *The Permanent Revolution: Apostolic Imagination and Practice for the 21st Century Church* (San Francisco: Jossey-Bass, 2012), xxxii–xxxiii.

2. Brent Curtis and John Eldredge, *The Sacred Romance: Drawing Closer to the Heart of God* (Nashville: Thomas Nelson, 1997), 41–43.

3. Will Mancini, *Church Unique: How Missional Leaders Cast Vision, Capture Culture, and Create Movement* (San Francisco: Jossey-Bass, 2008), 187–88.

4. I credit this insight to Dave Rhodes.

5. Metin Çakanyıldırım, "Nuclear Energy" (slide presentation), accessed March 7, 2020, https://personal.utdallas.edu/~metin/Merit/Folios/nuclear.pdf, 6.

6. G. Campbell Morgan, *The Westminster Pulpit Vol. III: The Preaching of G. Campbell Morgan* (Eugene, OR: Wipf & Stock, 2012), 27.

7. Warren Wiersbe, *Preaching and Teaching with Imagination: The Quest for Biblical Ministry* (Grand Rapids: Baker, 1994), chap. 5, NOOK.

8. Leonard Sweet, *Giving Blood: A Fresh Paradigm for Preaching* (Grand Rapids: Zondervan, 2014).

9. Carl F. George and Warren Bird, *How to Break Growth Barriers: Revise Your Role, Release Your People, and Capture Overlooked Opportunities for Your Church* (Grand Rapids: Baker Books, 2017), 88–89.

10. J. Robert Clinton, *The Making of a Leader: Recognizing the Lessons and Stages of Leadership Development* (Colorado Springs: NavPress, 1988), 200.

11. Kevin J. Vanhoozer, *Pictures at a Theological Exhibition: Scenes of the Church's Worship, Witness and Wisdom* (Downers Grove, IL: InterVarsity, 2016), introduction, NOOK.

Chapter 13 Funnel In: How the Assimilation Model Yields Diminished Returns

1. Frazee, *Connecting Church 2.0*; Jim Putman, *Real-Life Discipleship: Building Churches That Make Disciples* (Colorado Springs: NavPress, 2010); Greg L. Hawkins and Cally Parkinson, *Move: What 1,000 Churches Reveal about Spiritual Growth* (Grand Rapids: Zondervan, 2011).

2. Will Mancini, *Church Unique: How Missional Leaders Cast Vision, Capture Culture, and Create Movement* (San Francisco: Jossey-Bass, 2008), 113.

3. Simon Sinek, *Start with Why: How Great Leaders Inspire Everyone to Take Action* (New York: Penguin, 2009).

4. Paul Erdkamp, *The Grain Market in the Roman Empire: A Social, Political and Economic Study* (Cambridge, UK: Cambridge University Press, 2005), 42–46, https://books.google.com/books?id=IIj9uvGtJFEC.

Chapter 14 Funnel Out: How Jesus's Model Generated Multiplying Impact

1. Perhaps surprisingly, the difference between a two-year and a three-year length for Jesus's ministry hinges on a textual variant in John 5:1. Some manuscripts read that Jesus went up to Jerusalem for *"the* Feast of the Jews," which is almost certainly a reference to Passover. This would constitute a fourth Passover in Jesus's earthly ministry in addition to the three others clearly referred to in the Gospel of John. Other manuscripts, however, read *"a* feast of the Jews," which not only makes it possible but even probable that it was *not* the Passover. (The Pentecost following the Passover of John 2 is a good possibility, though this is speculative.) The editors of *The Greek New Testament*, 5th rev. ed. (also known as UBS5; Stuttgart: Deutsche Bibelgesellschaft, 2014) decisively favor "a feast of the Jews" as the original reading, a judgment followed by virtually all English translations. See also the footnote to John 5:1 in the NET Bible, https://www.bible gateway.com/passage/?search=john+5%3A1&version=NET.

2. For example, in Luke 4, Jesus's preaching in Nazareth is positioned as the first thing to happen in his ministry. But in the account, Jesus refers to miracles he had already performed in Capernaum (v. 23), which appear to be recounted later in the chapter.

3. We get hints of this in a few places. For example, after Jesus tells confusing parables to the crowd, "the Twelve *and the others around him* asked him about the parables" (Mark 4:10). That evening, Jesus takes disciples to the other side of the lake in a boat. A first-century Galilean boat could hold thirteen people rather snugly; nevertheless, "there were also other boats with him" (v. 36), most likely carrying more disciples.

4. Mark does not state where the feeding of the five thousand occurs, but he records that Jesus and his disciples go to Bethsaida *after* it takes place (Mark 6:45). The Gospel of John has them returning to Capernaum after the episode (John 6:17); Matthew says Gennesaret, three miles farther down the lakeshore from Capernaum (Matt. 14:34).

5. Matthew puts the same event earlier in Jesus's ministry (Matt. 8:18–22). The exact placement of this particular event is not important; what is important is Luke's indication that this sort of thing was still happening later in Jesus's ministry.

6. The textual evidence is evenly split between a reading of "seventy-two" and "seventy." Aside from the arguments for the authenticity of one or the other, I like seventy-two as a clean multiple of twelve, which in turn is echoed by 120 goers later.

Chapter 15 Funnel Fusion: How to Make Disciples without Abandoning the Institutional Presence of the Church in North America

1. Jeff Johnson, *Got Style?: Personality-Based Evangelism* (Valley Forge, PA: Judson Press, 2009), 135–46.

2. There is no single, universal format for the disciple-making vehicle called "discovery Bible study," but for information and examples see Final Command

Ministries, http://www.finalcommand.com; Neil Cole, *Church 3.0: Upgrades for the Future of the Church* (San Francisco: Jossey-Bass, 2010), chap. 8, NOOK; Roy Moran, *Spent Matches: Igniting the Signal Fire for the Spiritually Dissatisfied* (Nashville: Thomas Nelson, 2015), 121–40, 205–8.

3. Moran, *Spent Matches*, 97–119.

4. Michael Adam Beck, *Deep Roots, Wild Branches: Revitalizing the Church in the Blended Ecology* (Franklin, TN: Seedbed, 2019).

ABOUT THE AUTHORS

Will Mancini (ThM, Dallas Theological Seminary) is a church consultant and ministry entrepreneur. He started several interconnected organizations under The Future Church Co that help the church embody the movement that Jesus founded. Will's visionary planning tools, the Vision Frame and the Horizon Storyline, are used by thousands of churches every year through his calling to raise up other consultants and trainers. In 2015, he cofounded Younique to deliver gospel-centered life design through the church. In 2019, Will founded Denominee to help networks and denominations reinvent how they bring value to the church. He currently provides clarity and innovation consulting directly to church teams through Pivvot. He has written six books, including *Younique, Clarity Spiral, God Dreams, Innovating Discipleship*, and *Church Unique*. He enjoys speaking about how to live a life of more meaningful progress. Will lives in Houston with his wife, Romy, and has four children.

You can learn more about Will and his ecosystem of breakthrough ideas, tools, and organizations at www.willmancini.com. Connect with him on Instagram @will_be_clear and Twitter @willmancini.

Cory Hartman (DMin, Gordon-Conwell Theological Seminary) is the founder and principal writer of Fulcrum Content, a company that equips churches for disciple making and helps leaders extend their reach with the written word. He has collaborated on multiple books and authored two of his own.

Before founding Fulcrum, Cory served as a pastor for thirteen years. A native of central New York State, his family roots are in central Pennsylvania, where he now lives with his wife, Kelly, and their four children.